FEW AND CHOSEN

S SANTOP • ELSTON HOWARD • BUCK LEONARD •

YD • JACKIE ROBINSON • SAMMY T. HUGHES • NEWT

OP LLOYD • ERNIE BANKS • DICK LUNDY • JOHN

MARCELLE • JUD WILSON • HENRY THOMPSON • NEIL

MOROS • WILLARD BROWN • WILLIE MAYS • OSCAR

URKEY STEARNES • HENRY AARON • CRISTÓBAL

TCHFIELD • SMOKEY JOE WILLIAMS • SATCHEL PAIGE

ILLIE FOSTER • SLIM JONES • ROY PARTLOW • JOHN

DY TAYLOR • BUCK O'NEIL • VIC HARRIS • DAVE

SEY • EFFA MANLEY • ALEX POMPEZ • JOSH GIBSON •

TON HOWARD • BUCK LEONARD • GEORGE GILES •

OBINSON • SAMMY T. HUGHES • NEWT ALLEN • JIM

NIE BANKS • DICK LUNDY • JOHN BECKWITH • RAY

D WILSON • HENRY THOMPSON • NEIL ROBINSON •

RD BROWN • WILLIE MAYS • OSCAR CHARLESTON •

• HENRY AARON • CRISTÓBAL TORRIENTE • BILL

KEY JOE WILLIAMS • SATCHEL PAIGE • LEON DAY •

SLIM JONES • ROY PARTLOW • JOHN DONALDSON •

K O'NEIL • VIC HARRIS • DAVE MALARCHER • RUBE

FEW AND CHOSEN

Defining Negro Leagues Greatness

Monte Irvin
with Phil Pepe

TRIUMPH
B O O K S

Library of Congress Cataloging-in-Publication Data

Irvin, Monte, 1919–
     Few and chosen : defining Negro leagues greatness / Monte Irvin with Phil Pepe.
        p. cm.
     Includes bibliographical references and index.
     ISBN-13: 978-1-57243-855-2 (alk. paper)
     ISBN-10: 1-57243-855-X (alk. paper)
     1. Negro leagues—History. 2. Baseball—United States—History. 3. African American baseball players—History. 4. Discrimination in sports—United States—History. I. Pepe, Phil. II. Title.

GV875.N35I79 2007
796.357'6408996073—dc22

                                                                                 2006032037

This book is available in quantity at special discounts for your group or organization. For further information, contact:

Triumph Books
542 South Dearborn Street
Suite 750
Chicago, Illinois 60605
(312) 939-3330
Fax (312) 663-3557

Printed in U.S.A.
ISBN: 978-1-57243-855-2
Design by Nick Panos; page production by Patricia Frey
All photos courtesy of the National Baseball Hall of Fame Library, Cooperstown, New York, unless otherwise indicated

Monte Irvin's Hall of Fame induction speech on pages xxvii–xxviii is reprinted with permission of the National Baseball Hall of Fame Library. Branch Rickey's remarks on pages 36–38 appeared in *Baseball Has Done It,* copyright by Jack R. Robinson and Charles Dexter and published by J.B. Lippincott Company in 1964. Publisher has made every effort to obtain permission to reprint this piece.

This book is affectionately and gratefully dedicated to all those who blazed the trail in the Negro Leagues but never got the chance to display their enormous talents on the national stage—the major leagues—players like Pop Lloyd, Biz Mackey, Josh Gibson, "Smokey" Joe Williams, Buck Leonard, Leon Day, Willie Wells, Oscar Charleston, Cool Papa Bell, Ray Dandridge, "Double Duty" Radcliffe, and dozens of others.

It is also dedicated to those who had the courage and the foresight to make it finally happen…

To Jackie Robinson, Branch Rickey, Clyde Sukeforth, Commissioner A.B. "Happy" Chandler, Commissioner Bowie Kuhn, Commissioner Fay Vincent, Bob Feller, and Ted Williams, who first called for the inclusion of Negro Leagues players in the Hall of Fame during his induction speech in 1966.

And finally, it is written in loving memory of John Jordan "Buck" O'Neil (1911–2006).

Dedicated to Negro League Baseball

(Oh how)
I wish I could've seen
My brothers play ball
With
That ole negro league
I mean
To really get down
On that coppered colored diamond
And
Pitch a no-hitter
With Flamin' Satchel or Slim Jones
To see a whole crowd
Of Colored folk
A jumpin' and a hollerin'
Holding dey babies
With men grittin'
Ivory stained cigar teeth gambling
(screaming)
Popcorn!!!
Peanuts!!!
Admission?
Boy
Don't you know it's free to see
Buck O'Neil's watchful eye on the plate
Buggin' it
Right out of the park
Or
Leon Day's smile speckle sunshine
On a gray and cloudy afternoon.
Remember that?
Reckon not.
But I wish
I could've seen
My brothers
PLAY BALL!

—Stewart Lee Stone

Stewart Lee Stone of Lexington, Kentucky, a recent graduate of Berea (Kentucky) College, was born some 30 years after the Negro Leagues folded. As a youngster, he developed an interest in African American culture and became fascinated with Negro Leagues baseball after reading a children's book on the subject.

His poem, "Dedicated to Negro League Baseball," was written when he was 17 years old and earned him the prestigious 2005 Francis S. Hutchins Award from Berea College.

Contents

Preface

It had to have been a holiday. If April 10, 1947, was a Thursday and there was no school (I never would dare play hooky), it must have been the Easter recess. What I do remember is that it was three weeks past my 12th birthday, and my brother Paul, two and a half years my senior, and I took advantage of the break in school to go to a baseball game.

It was only an exhibition game, the Dodgers against their Triple A International League farm team, the Montreal Royals, but any chance to see our beloved Dodgers was a treat.

Armed with a bagful of Mom's sandwiches, we made the 45-minute journey by train, walked past Prospect Park and the Botanical Garden, past the Bond Bread sign, and arrived at Ebbets Field where we purchased our customary bleacher seats, 60¢ each.

I have no recollection of what happened in the game, who won, or whether there were any home runs or any sensational catches.

One thing I recall is that even from as far away as the bleachers, it was apparent that the only black player on either team was a Montreal infielder named Jackie Robinson. I was not enlightened enough to comprehend the historical significance of that, or of the report in the next day's newspaper that the Dodgers had purchased the contract of that same Jackie Robinson and that he would be in their starting lineup against the Boston Braves for the season opener five days later.

In the early days of the new season, I closely monitored—through box scores in the newspaper and by listening to games on the radio—the new man's performance. I rooted hard for Jackie Robinson to succeed, not out of any social consciousness, or because I wanted baseball to right its wrongs of the previous 50 years, or in the spirit of equality and fair play, or because I was aware of the enormous pressure he was under and the threats he endured to his physical well-being, or because of the bigoted verbal attacks he faced from opposing players and even from some of his teammates who protested his presence and threatened to boycott the team rather than play alongside him. At 12 years old, what did I know about racial injustice? My reason for rooting for Robinson was a basic and selfish one. He was a Dodger, and I wanted him to do well, to hit and field and run and help my Dodgers win their first pennant in six years.

In my neighborhood, we rarely saw a black person. There was one man who worked on a coal truck, and he came to deliver coal to the houses on my street.

In the eighth grade I had a black classmate. His name was Paul Williams, and he lived about 10 blocks away from me. We weren't very close. I never invited him to my home, and I was never invited to his, but he played third base on my sandlot baseball team, and we were happy to have him because he was a good player.

The adults in my neighborhood were divided into those who were anti-Robinson and those who were pro-Robinson. Those who were Dodgers fans rooted for Robinson; those who were fans of other teams rooted against him, even one in my own household. My father wanted Robinson to fail, because my father was a Giants fan. When the Giants acquired Henry Thompson, Willie Mays, and Monte Irvin, Dad rooted hard for them. Monte Irvin was my father's favorite player.

In youthful innocence, and ignorance, I never questioned why there were no black players in the major leagues. If I thought about it at all, I suppose I simply concluded that they were not good enough to play for the Dodgers, or the Yankees, or the Giants.

My opinion changed after African Americans entered the major leagues. I marveled at the skill, the power, the speed, the defensive brilliance of Larry Doby and Luke Easter with the Indians; Ernie Banks, Gene Baker, and George Altman with the Cubs; George Crowe with the Reds; Hank Aaron and Sam Jethroe with the Braves; Thompson, Mays, and Irvin with the Giants; and, of course, Jackie Robinson, Roy Campanella, and Don Newcombe with my Dodgers.

I had heard stories about the incredible ability of players from the Negro Leagues, like Josh Gibson, Buck Leonard, Oscar Charleston, Willie Wells, Pop Lloyd, Ray Dandridge, Judy Johnson, Cool Papa Bell, Leon Day, Martin Dihigo, Smokey Williams, Cannonball Redding, Willie Foster, and the legendary, ageless wonder, Satchel Paige—all men who were denied their rightful place alongside Babe Ruth, Lou Gehrig, Joe DiMaggio, Ted Williams, Bob Feller, and Lefty Grove.

And we were denied the pleasure of watching them.

At first I thought those stories were mere hyperbole, but years later, when I became a baseball writer for a New York newspaper, I had the opportunity to talk to people who had seen these men play, who had played with them and against them, and I learned that those stories were not hyperbole at all.

Given the chance, would Josh Gibson have hit more than 60 home runs in a season?

Would Satchel Paige have won 300 games? Pitched several no-hitters?

Would Cool Papa Bell have been the first man to steal 100 bases?

Sadly, we'll never know.

Happily, we have Monte Irvin to enlighten us. Talking with him is like taking a trip through the history of Negro Leagues baseball. He remembers attending Negro Leagues games as a boy and later was a member of the Newark Eagles, from 1938 through 1948, with time out for military service and a year in the Mexican Summer League, playing with, or against, all of the great players of that exceptional era of Negro Leagues baseball. With a natural curiosity and inquisitiveness and a strong sense of ethnic pride, he learned about those who came before him from older teammates, and he carried those stories and memories with him all these years with a recall that is astounding.

I remembered Monte Irvin from the 1951 season, a player I feared, respected, and hated. He was, after all, a New York Giant. He batted .312 that year with 24 home runs and a league-leading 121 runs batted in. He should have been the National League Most Valuable Player. Roy Campanella was. Irvin finished third in the voting.

I got to know Monte some years later when he worked in the office of Commissioner Bowie Kuhn. I came to appreciate and admire him as a man of great dignity and humility. A man you can trust.

I trust Monte Irvin.

Black baseball teams go back as far as the 1880s, but it wasn't until 1920 that the Negro National League came into being—later to be joined briefly by the Eastern Colored League and the Negro American League—and it lasted into the early 1950s. It's that 30-plus-year period that gets our attention here.

Record keeping from the Negro Leagues was sketchy at best and difficult to corroborate. But records don't matter. What does matter is personal observation, so I'll trust Monte to accept the challenge of picking the all-time team from the halcyon days of Negro Leagues baseball.

Who better to take on this monumental task than my father's favorite ballplayer?

—Phil Pepe

Introduction

All these years later, I still remember that day so clearly—October 23, 1945, a day that would change my life and the lives of many like me, a day that would have a profound and lasting impact on the game of baseball and, indeed, on the American way of life.

I had recently completed another season with the Newark Eagles in the Negro National League when word came that the Brooklyn Dodgers had signed Jack Roosevelt Robinson, an African American, to a professional baseball contract.

I remember feeling joy, and a touch of sadness, too. I remember the mixed emotions, the feeling of hope, and of despair—hope because it meant that, finally, black men would have the opportunity to show their baseball ability on the game's greatest stage, the major leagues. We knew what it was going to mean to hundreds of young African American baseball players in the future, and we were all rooting hard for Jackie to succeed. But there also was despair, because we knew that if Jackie succeeded, it would lead to the demise of the Negro Leagues, and a lot of the older players would be out of a job.

I was exhilarated at the news for myself and for other young men who were my contemporaries and those that would come after us, because now we had a chance that we thought never would come. I was only 26 years old at the time, still young enough to look forward to several productive years in baseball, my prime years.

At the same time I was saddened for men like John Beckwith, Martin Dihigo, Bingo DeMoss, Willie Foster, Louis Santop, George Giles, Pop

Lloyd, Newt Allen, Judy Johnson, Turkey Stearnes, "Smokey" Joe Williams, and Slim Jones, whose time had come and gone. And for Josh Gibson, Willie Wells, Ray Dandridge, Cool Papa Bell, Oscar Charleston, Leon Day, Buck Leonard, and Satchel Paige, whose best years were behind them.

That's progress: unfortunately, you can't have it both ways.

I entered the world on February 25, 1919, in Haleburg, Alabama, the third youngest of the 11 children—five girls and six boys—of Cupid Alexander Irvin and Mary Eliza Henderson Irvin. My folks named me Montford Merrill, but there was no significance to the name Montford. I guess they read it in a book and liked the name.

My daddy—everybody called him C.A.—who was born in 1878 during Rutherford B. Hayes's administration, owned 300 acres, and he farmed the land: cotton, pecans, peanuts, and sugarcane. He had his own mill where he ground up the cane into juice, which he boiled off to make molasses.

Dad lived until he was 85 years old, and I'm happy that he was around long enough to see me play for the New York Giants. He loved that, coming to the Polo Grounds and meeting Leo Durocher and all the players.

My mother was a teacher. In those days in the South, if you could read a little better than everybody else, they made you a teacher. She taught until she married my father, and then they had one child after another, and that was the end of her teaching career. My mother was born in 1882, and she lived until she was 87, so we were blessed with good genes in our family. I had two sisters who lived until they were 89, and my second-oldest sister, Nonnie, was 96 when she passed away.

Even though he had no formal education, my father could read and write, and he and my mother instilled in us the importance of education. My father was very supportive. He told us that education was the best thing we could have, and he encouraged us to get as much schooling as we could.

Besides good genes, I figure we Irvins also inherited our athletic ability from our father, who was a pretty good baseball player. All the farmers in and around Haleburg would work a half day on Saturday, and after they finished work, they'd gather and choose up sides and play baseball. The women prepared food, and the men played baseball and drank cane juice and just had a good time. The farmers had worked hard all week, so Saturday was their time to enjoy themselves and have some fun playing baseball before it got dark.

The Irvin boys all became proficient in sports. My brother Bob could throw as hard as anybody who ever lived, but he never pursued baseball. My brother Milton, who went to Virginia State, was more into football than any other sport. Another brother, Calvin, who was the youngest in the family and who was named after President Coolidge, was a terrific baseball player. He played two years for the Newark Eagles and was an excellent shortstop. He could outrun me, and he had a better arm than I had. But he told me, "Monte, I'm just a singles and doubles hitter. There's no future for me in baseball; I'm going to go to college and get my degree because I want to coach and teach."

And he did. He went to Morgan State at the same time as Joe Black, who later pitched for the Brooklyn Dodgers and was Rookie of the Year in the National League in 1952. Cal had never played football, not even in high school, but at Morgan they asked him to go out for the football team because he was on an athletic scholarship.

"But I got the scholarship for basketball," Cal said.

"We know," they said, "but give us a hand; we need football players."

Cal agreed to go out for football, and he made all-conference in the Colored Intercollegiate Athletic Association (CIAA)—that's how good of an athlete he was. He played three years of basketball, but in his third year he hurt his knee, and in his senior year, he told the coach, "I don't think I'll play this year. My knee is swelling, and I don't want to hurt it and be crippled for life."

"You have to play," the coach said. "You're on scholarship."

Cal said, "Coach, I don't have to play, and I'm not playing."

"If you don't," the coach said, "you'll lose your scholarship."

"That's all right," Cal said, and he transferred to the University of Illinois for his senior year and got his degree there. After he graduated, he got a job teaching in a high school in Charlotte, North Carolina, where he stayed a few years and then became basketball coach, and later athletics director, at North Carolina A&T State University in Greensboro. (Editor's note: Calvin Coolidge Irvin, recently retired, won 401 basketball games and five CIAA championships at North Carolina A&T. He was elected to the North Carolina Sports Hall of Fame in 1988.)

Life was difficult for black families in rural Alabama in the 1920s. We lived among white families, and we all got along, but there was a separation, and there was only so much a black man could accomplish. There were segregated buses, segregated restrooms, segregated restaurants, segregated everything. My older brother and sister had to walk three or four miles to get to school. The bus carrying the white kids to the same school would pass them on the road. It was half empty, but the driver wouldn't stop to give my brother and sister a ride. At that time, integration was illegal in Alabama.

With the crops my father produced, we always had enough to eat and enough money to get by, but there was a man named Buck Carter who ran the town's general store, and my father patronized Carter's General Store for food, seed, and supplies. Carter would keep a record of what we bought, and we'd settle up at the end of the month, all on the honor system. When it came time to pay the bill, our records would show one figure and Carter's would always be twice as much. Whatever he said we owed, that was it. There was no haggling. It was "this is it, see you later, Charlie."

Eventually, my father got tired of such treatment, and that's when he decided to move the family north, because in the South the playing field wasn't level. I was eight years old at the time.

The record books say I was born in Columbia, Alabama, not Haleburg. Let me explain. When we moved to New Jersey, as a kind of silent protest because my father was treated so poorly in Haleburg, we told people we came from Columbia, which is seven miles away from Haleburg (Dothan, 12 miles away, is the nearest big town).

Years later the town of Haleburg held a dinner in my honor. I was reluctant to attend at first, but then I decided to let bygones be bygones. I returned to Haleburg, and I'm glad I did. It was a wonderful tribute. The people couldn't have been nicer. When I got up to speak, I said, "I hope you forgive me for saying I was born in Columbia. Now that the playing field is more even, I'm reclaiming Haleburg as my birthplace."

At the dinner, I met the grandnephew of Buck Carter, the man who had cheated my father. We shook hands, had our picture taken together, and buried the hatchet. People kept apologizing for what happened in the past. "We're sorry it was that way back then, but that's how it was at the time," that sort of thing. At least things got better there, and it's even better now. Race relations in that part of the country are so much better today than they were when I was a boy.

We settled in New Jersey because my oldest sister, Pearl, had married and moved there. She rented a big house for us in Bloomfield, and we moved into that house: all of us in that one big house.

Things were much better for us in New Jersey than they were in Alabama. My father was very good with horses from his days on the farm, and he took a job with Becker's Dairy, a wonderful milk company that had been in business 35 or 40 years. The milkmen would make their deliveries by horse and wagon, and my father tended the horses: cleaned, groomed, and fed them and cleaned the stables. He always worked steadily but never made more than $15 per week.

We lived in Bloomfield, and the dairy was in Orange, about 10 miles away. In those days, that area was all farmland. That land became very valuable, and today the farms have been replaced by condominiums and shopping centers.

Our family didn't have a car back then, so my father would take a street car to and from work, and it would take him anywhere from a half hour to an hour each way. Somebody said, "Why don't you just move to Orange?" We did, and then my father was able to walk to work.

The schools in New Jersey were integrated, so I grew up going to class and competing in sports with white kids who outnumbered blacks by about six to one.

I was very energetic when I was a youngster. I was always running, jumping, throwing. I also had an interest in music. I had heard Lester Young playing with the Count Basie band, and I wanted to play tenor sax like Lester, so I asked my mother to lend me $5 so I could put a down payment on a tenor sax. I took the $5 and was on my way to the music store when I passed a Davega sporting goods store, where I saw this beautiful baseball glove in the window. Instead of going to the music store, I went in and bought the glove.

Who knows? If I hadn't passed the sporting goods store, I might have become another Lester Young.

The lure of sports was greater for me than the lure of music, especially after I discovered that I could beat all the kids my age in just about every sport. I started out as a soccer player in grade school, and one day my carpentry shop teacher, who also was a coach, said, "Monte, baseball season is coming. Why don't you go out for the team?"

I did, and they made me a pitcher because I could throw harder and better than any of the other kids. I'd pitch a game, and then I'd have to sit out for three or four days. I didn't like that, so I started to catch because I wanted to be involved in every play. But we had one kid on the team who couldn't play any position other than catcher, so I moved to shortstop so he could catch.

At Orange High School I was all-state in four sports: baseball, football, basketball, and track. In baseball I batted .667 my senior year, and one of my teachers had a contact with the Yankees, so he called his contact and told him about me, but the Yankees never contacted me.

In track and field I threw the shot put, and I broke the New Jersey state record in the javelin.

Football was my best sport. I was a natural in football. I could run, and I loved to tackle. (We played both ways in those days; I was a running back on offense and a linebacker on defense.) I was offered a scholarship to the University of Michigan for football, but in February of my senior year, I got a streptococcus infection. I had three operations, and I was hospitalized for six weeks. Because of my illness, Michigan withdrew my scholarship. Our family doctor, Dr. William Davis, said, "Monte, if you want to go to college, I can get you a four-year scholarship to Lincoln College [now university, in Oxford, Pennsylvania]."

I spent a year and a half at Lincoln, which is the alma mater of Supreme Court Justice Thurgood Marshall, and played baseball, basketball, and football there and still threw the javelin. In football, I was a triple offensive threat—kicking, passing, and running. I played linebacker on defense, and I made All-CIAA. But I quit school because of a disagreement with the athletics director, and I decided to devote all of my time to baseball.

Although football was my best sport, I was a big baseball fan thanks to my brother Bob, who fostered my love for baseball. Bob rooted for the Philadelphia Athletics, which had a powerhouse team in the 1930s. He loved Jimmie Foxx, Lefty Grove, George Earnshaw, and Connie Mack. He even became a pen pal of Connie Mack's. He'd write Mack letters, and Mack would write him back. Bob would save up his money, and when he had enough, he'd go to Philadelphia by train to see the Athletics play. He'd take me with him, and I became an A's fan, too. Bob loved baseball. Every week he'd buy *The Sporting News* for 10¢ and read about his Athletics.

Bob and I worked during the summer and after school, and we'd save up our money and—about two or three times a year—when we had saved $2 apiece, we'd make the trip from Orange across the Hudson River to the Bronx to see the Yankees play.

On Memorial Day 1938, we went to Yankee Stadium for a doubleheader between the Yankees and the Boston Red Sox. Lefty Grove pitched for Boston against Red Ruffing in the first game, and Lefty Gomez pitched for the Yankees in the second game. We bought standing-room-only tickets because in those days they let you sit in the aisles (later the fire department put a stop to that practice). That day the crowd was an all-time record (Editor's note: official attendance was 81,841). By then I had become a big Joe DiMaggio fan. I had never seen anything like him: graceful, classic stance, classic swing.

Even though my brother Bob and I would go to Philadelphia or Yankee Stadium as often as we could, we saw more Negro Leagues games than major league ones because the tickets were cheaper and the games were closer to home. The Negro Leagues teams would come to play the white team in East Orange, and I got to see all the great Negro Leagues stars of that time: Josh Gibson, Satchel Paige, Buck Leonard, and many others. I started following the Newark Eagles because that was the Negro National League team that was closest to my home.

After I left Lincoln College I started getting offers to play in the Negro National League. At the time there was no future in football or basketball, especially for blacks. At least in the Negro Leagues, I figured, I could make a little money. *Very little.*

I got an offer to play for the Homestead Grays and another from a team in Brooklyn, but Abe and Effa Manley, who owned the Newark Eagles, came at me hard. Their strongest pitch was that if I signed with Newark, I could live at home and save money. They played that up.

"If you sign with us," they said, "you can save that road rent."

"I need to save all the money I can," I said, "because with what you're offering, I'm sure not going to be making much money here."

"Mr. Manley," I said, "I like the Eagles, and I'd sure like to sign with you, but what about some kind of bonus?"

He said, "You should be happy and proud to play with the Eagles. We don't give bonuses."

I told him the Homestead Grays were interested, and he said, "You don't want to play with them; they travel too much. You're young [I was only 19], and you have a chance to make some decent money in time."

In time!

"Mr. Manley," I said, "what about *now*? I'd like to help my mother and father with expenses."

"I can't do anything like that now," Manley said, "but if you turn out to be a pretty good player, maybe I can give you a little something extra later on."

I signed with the Eagles for $125 per month, largely because I could save money by living at home with my parents. I had a pretty good year, and, sure enough, that Christmas I got a check in the mail with a note that said, "We didn't give you a bonus, but for playing so great for us, here's $50."

Before World War II, the average salary in the Negro Leagues was $200 per month. Even the biggest stars didn't make much more than that, but when you consider that the average working person in the United States was making about $10 or $15 per week, if you made $40 or $50 per week playing baseball, that wasn't so bad—you were ahead of the game.

We'd also get a-dollar-a-day meal money, and in those days, you could eat well for a dollar a day. You could get dinner—an entrée, two vegetables, iced tea, and dessert—for 30¢. The club paid for lodgings, such as they were, on the road, but at home you had to assume your own expenses. So what some of the guys did was rent an apartment and double and triple up to save on expenses. I was living with my parents, so it didn't cost me anything, but I did contribute to the household expenses.

When I signed with Newark, I still had college eligibility remaining, and I thought if I didn't make it with the Eagles, I could always go back to college. In order to protect my eligibility, I played away games only, using the name Jimmy Nelson. I picked that name because Jimmy Nelson was a catcher and I started out as a catcher in high school. Nelson had a great physique and looked good in a uniform, so I figured, how could I go wrong?

At home I worked out with the team before the game, and when the game started, I took a seat in the stands and watched. Communications back then weren't what they are today. I could play on the road under a different name and nobody would notice. Everybody did it, including Jim Thorpe. But at home I was known, and I was afraid that if I tried playing in Newark, somebody would report me and I'd lose my amateur standing.

With the Eagles I started out as a third baseman. I also worked out at shortstop with Willie Wells, a terrific player and the Eagles' star shortstop. One day during infield practice, Willie said, "Monte, with your speed and your arm, your position is out there," and he pointed to center field.

"I don't care where I play," I said. "I just want to play."

That's how I became an outfielder.

Later, after Wells left, the Eagles moved me to shortstop, and that's the position I played when we won the Negro Leagues World Series in 1946. The second baseman, my double-play partner, was a 21-year-old kid from Paterson, New Jersey, named Larry Doby.

Early on I had trouble hitting the curveball and also pulling the ball. I would hit everything to the opposite field—line drives to right field. So I'd go to Yankee Stadium as often as I could to watch DiMaggio and study how he hit. He had a dead left leg, and he just turned the bat over and hit the ball hard to left field.

In 1942 we had spring training in Daytona Beach, and I spent a lot of time that spring working on DiMaggio's style of hitting. I practiced picking my left leg up and putting it back in the same spot and turning the bat over like DiMaggio did. Anything from the middle of the plate out, I would take back through the middle, but if the ball was from the middle of the plate in, I would turn on it and pull it to left field. I did that over and over, and by the time spring training ended, I had it down pat.

I discovered that by using that style I could pull the fastball by turning the bat over, I could hit the curveball by catching it during the break or after the break, and I could hit the change-up by staying back and waiting for the ball instead of lunging at it. I had found my style of hitting.

When I first started, teams would pitch me inside, because if you're a right-handed hitter who hits the ball to right field, they'll try to jam you. In 1942, when I went to Mexico, pitchers were still pitching me inside, and I would hit that ball to left field. I went the whole year before pitchers got wise to the fact that I was now a pull hitter, and I batted .397 that season.

Playing in the Negro Leagues was a challenge. Except for an occasional game in a major league ballpark, the fields were generally rock piles, and lighting for night games was not what it is today. We played uneven schedules, and we didn't have adequate medical attention or training facilities. We didn't have any coaching to speak of. If you didn't know how to do something, you'd talk it over with one of the major leaguers you got friendly with during barnstorming games. Or you might get help from a teammate, but sometimes a teammate would be reluctant to help you for fear that you would take his job. For the most part, we were self-taught, and we learned by trial and error.

Hotel accommodations, when we got them, were second class. Travel was rough, with long rides on rickety buses. The bus was practically our home. Most guys said they could sleep better on the bus than they did in a bed because we spent more time on the bus. After a game, we would climb aboard the bus, hang our uniforms outside the window to dry, and head for the next town.

Conditions were abominable, but we didn't know any better. We had nothing to compare them to. We were young and strong, and we loved the game so much. We were playing as well as we could, but because of the conditions, we were probably playing at no more than 75 percent of our ability. There's no telling how good these guys could have been with better playing conditions.

We'd play the Negro Leagues season, and then, after the season, some of us would go on barnstorming tours or off to the Winter Leagues in Mexico, Cuba, and Puerto Rico—wherever we could earn the most money. We'd play baseball 10, 11 months a year.

In Puerto Rico a couple of kids latched on to me. They'd carry my bag into the ballpark and run errands for me if I needed something. They became my protégés, and later they became my good friends. Their names were Roberto Clemente and Orlando Cepeda.

There were some major leaguers playing winter ball in Mexico, Cuba, and Puerto Rico, and occasionally, some of the Negro Leagues players would talk about getting a chance to play in the major leagues. You'd hear them say, "Why can't they give me a chance? I want to know how good I am. I want to compete against the best. I want to know if I can hit Dizzy Dean and Walter Johnson; if I can hit Red Ruffing, Lefty Gomez, and Lefty Grove."

We were frustrated. You'd look around and see blacks coexisting with whites in other areas. In boxing, Joe Louis, John Henry Lewis, and Henry Armstrong were world champions, the idols of thousands. They'd fight against white fighters in front of primarily white audiences with no incidents.

In music, Benny Goodman integrated his band with Lionel Hampton and Teddy Wilson and played at Carnegie Hall in front of largely white audiences, again without incident. But baseball continued to operate in the dark ages. The owners were so against integrating the major leagues that we figured it would never happen.

We held our own against major leaguers in winter ball and when we barnstormed against them. We showed that even though we played in the Negro Leagues, we were capable of playing good baseball. We got to be friendly with some of the white players, and we knew we had their respect and their support, so we'd ask them, "Why don't you guys talk it up? We'd like to play. Maybe we can help you win a pennant." And they'd say, "We'll do what we can, but it's up to the owners."

That's the way it was until Jackie Robinson played with Montreal in 1946. Until then, we just accepted the way things were and figured we'd never get our chance.

When I worked in the office of baseball commissioner Bowie Kuhn, I served on a committee with Shirley Povich, the outstanding sportswriter from Washington, D.C. The Homestead Grays had moved some of their games to Washington in 1938, so I asked Shirley about it.

I had heard that Senators owner Clark Griffith could sit in his office and look out and see the field and that he watched Buck Leonard and Josh Gibson belting the ball all over the lot. In 1943 Gibson hit 10 home runs in Griffith Stadium. In one game that season, he blasted three home runs, including one that landed two feet from the top of the left-center-field bleachers, 485 feet away from home plate. Griffith had to be impressed, and tempted, especially with his team perennially at the bottom of the American League. As they used to say, "Washington: first in war, first in peace, and last in the American League."

Povich said he once asked Griffith, "Clark, have you ever thought about signing Gibson, Leonard, Roy Partlow, and Raymond Brown, four stars? You could sign those players for no bonus, and they might move you up from last place to first."

According to Povich, Griffith replied, "I have businesses in the South. If I did that, I couldn't go back home."

"You would be known for your humanitarianism," Povich said.

"Well, somebody else will have to do it," Griffith said. "I can't do it."

Griffith actually called Leonard and Gibson up to his office and talked to them about playing for the Senators, but he never did make them an offer.

Another time, I was talking with a baseball executive, and I said, "You sent your scouts out to watch us play, and we played with the same gloves, the same ball, the same bats, the same rules, and we played great against each other. Why didn't you think we could play great against major leaguers?"

"That was our mind-set," this executive said. "It was wrong, I know it was wrong, but that's the way we felt at that time."

That was the frustration black players felt in the early days. Take Biz Mackey, the great catcher who was my manager and mentor with the Newark Eagles. He told me that when he was playing with the Baltimore Elite Giants, where he first met Roy Campanella, after the season, they would barnstorm against major league teams. Starting about the first of October, they'd play about 30 games against the Philadelphia Phillies, the Philadelphia Athletics, and other major league teams intact and, without any formal instruction and coaching, the Elite Giants would win a good percentage of those games.

So if they acquitted themselves well in those barnstorming games against major league teams, why didn't the major league owners think they could play the same way in the major leagues?

In Newark I was doing well, living at home and enjoying playing with the Eagles, and then I got an offer to play in the Mexican Summer League. I was making $150 per month with the Eagles, but they were offering me $700 per month, almost five times my Newark salary, to play in Mexico, plus an apartment and a maid. I went to Effa Manley, who was running the Eagles for her husband, Abe, and I told her about the offer.

"I can't approach that, Monte," Effa said. "You'll just have to go."

"I hate to leave this great team," I told her, "but I need more money, I'm planning to get married."

So I took the offer from Mexico. They sent me an advance of $1,000, more money than I had ever seen in my life, and Dee and I got married in New Jersey and took off for Mexico City for a working honeymoon.

I missed winning the Triple Crown by two RBIs. A great Cuban player named Silvio Garcia beat me out, but I batted .397 on my honeymoon.

Mexico City was a terrific place. I loved it. They had rebuilt the city after an earthquake, and it was just wonderful there—new theaters; new hotels; new restaurants; big, wide streets; great weather; just a wonderful place to play. I got away from the cold weather, made some money, and learned to speak Spanish.

After the season, I was drafted into the army, and I reported to Fort Dix, New Jersey, on March 9, 1943, and was sent to Fort Belvoir, Virginia, for basic training. After basic training I was sent to Camp Claiborne, Louisiana, for a few months. I spent three years with the General Service Engineers and was sent to France, England, and Germany, but I never saw any action.

When I was discharged in 1945, the Dodgers offered me a contract. I hadn't played baseball in three years, I had a rough time in the army, and I didn't think I was ready. I told the Dodgers I needed to get the old feeling again. I didn't want to fail, so I declined the offer, went to play in Puerto Rico, and then rejoined the Newark Eagles.

Looking back now, I wonder if I could have been the first African American to play in the major leagues.

Would I have wanted to be the first?

onte Irvin reached the pinnacle of his profession on August 6, 1973, when—along with umpire Billy Evans; 19th-century pitcher Mickey Welch; Long George "Highpockets" Kelly; Warren Spahn, the winningest left-hander in baseball history; and the then recently deceased Roberto Clemente—he was inducted into the National Baseball Hall of Fame in Cooperstown, New York.

While introducing Irvin, Commissioner Bowie Kuhn said, "Goodness knows what he might have achieved in addition to what he achieved in the major leagues had he been able to come and spend those 10 or 12 earlier years with us in the majors. And never, do I feel, has baseball produced a kinder, more decent, more beloved man, or one who has meant more to me personally than Monte Irvin."

Following is Irvin's acceptance speech.

As most of you know, I'd rather face Warren Spahn than make a speech, so I beg your indulgence. I've been coming to this historical place for many years. When I was a member of the New York Giants and when I was a member of the Chicago Cubs, I played in the ceremonial games. Only last year I was sitting out there in the audience and now I'm up here among those to be honored as a tribute to baseball, and it gives me a feeling that I cannot describe.

I never saw some of the old-timers, but I read about Long George Kelly, one of the most versatile players to ever put on a uniform. And, of course, Warren Spahn who was the toughest left-hander that I ever faced. And, of course, my real good friend Roberto Clemente for hitting, for fielding, for throwing, for hitting with power, for hitting for high average, one of the greatest that ever did it. I met Roberto many years back in Puerto Rico, and we became real close friends. To be so honored up here today with these men and all of the rest of the Hall of Famers gives me a feeling that I just cannot describe, and the only thing I can say, it is just the greatest in the world. You know, I played in the bus leagues for many years, overworked, underpaid, but somehow now this does not seem to be in vain. And I hope my induction will help ease the pain of all of those players who never got a chance to play in the majors.

I wish my father could be here today, because he was a great baseball fan. He passed away a few years ago, but when I was growing up he was always there to give me a word of encouragement and say the right thing to keep me going. He would have certainly enjoyed being here and sharing this honor with me. However, my two daughters, Pam and Patti, are here, and my wife, Dee. And I'd just like for them to stand up and take a bow, and also Patti's young man, Craig Gordon.

It is often said that a person is real lucky when he has one or two true friends. Well, many years ago when I attended Lincoln University, in my freshman year I met a man named Ernie Young, and he and his wife are here today, and believe me ladies and gentlemen, they are true friends. Thelma and Ernie Young, would you please stand up. Other friends of mine have come great distances, and I deeply appreciate them being here.

Finally, I received many thrills in baseball. I remember the 1951 miracle year of the New York Giants. I remember all the honors I have received in Puerto Rico, Mexico, Venezuela, and Cuba, but none can equal the great feeling, wonderful marvelous feeling that I have right now. It is the greatest I've ever had. Thank you.

I would have loved that opportunity, but the timing was not right for me. I know how tough it was for Jackie Robinson, what he went through, and I have often wondered if I would have been able to endure what he did. I have no doubt I would have.

I had experienced prejudice as a boy in Alabama and later traveling in the South with the Eagles. We faced segregation, and we heard all the words, but as long as you didn't abuse me physically, I could stand almost anything. I don't think I would have had a problem.

One time I was barnstorming on a team of black major leaguers—Larry Doby, Ernie Banks, Luke Easter, and Roy Campanella as manager—and we had a game in Columbus, Mississippi.

We were staying in a black hotel, and after a game, our first baseman, Len Pearson, went up to his room to call his wife back home. The hotel telephone operator wouldn't put his call through because he wouldn't say "yes ma'am" to her.

Campanella asked him, "What did you say to her, Lenny?"

Pearson said, "I told her to take the telephone and shove it."

"You said what?" Campy screeched.

Our bus was on the street, right outside the hotel, and once we heard that, all of us went to our rooms, got our bags, and got on the bus and told the bus driver to take off. We heard later on that the Ku Klux Klan and the police came to the hotel and wanted to know who the guy was that sassed the telephone operator.

Even in the army, I faced bigotry. I was with a black unit, and I remember being on a train going to Louisiana. We went to the dining car to eat, and they put us in a booth, and some guy came by and closed the curtains to separate us from the rest of the dining room.

"Hey, man," we said. "We're in the army like everybody else, fighting for our country. Do you have to close the curtain?"

"I know how you feel, but that's the law," he said.

That's the way it was. We were treated better in France, England, and Germany than we were in the United States. You couldn't help asking yourself, "What are we fighting for?"

So, yes, I faced a lot of the same stuff that Jackie Robinson faced when he joined the Dodgers, and I'm sure I could have tolerated it. I would love to have been the first, but how can you argue with the job Jackie did? As it turned out, they picked the right person when they picked Jackie Robinson to break the color line.

My biggest regret is that integration in baseball didn't come 10 years earlier than it did. If it had, they could have had the cream of the crop from the Negro Leagues, guys like Buck Leonard and Josh Gibson, Willie Wells and Ray Dandridge. They could have had Sam Jethroe and Satchel Paige in their prime.

It's those great players I honor here by picking my all-time team from the Negro Leagues, with this disclaimer: some of the players on my team, like Jackie Robinson, Henry Aaron, Willie Mays, Larry Doby, and Elston Howard, played only briefly in the Negro Leagues, but I chose them based on what I believe they would have accomplished had they continued playing in the Negro Leagues and what they did accomplish in the major leagues.

I have limited my selections to those I saw play or those I heard about from my contemporaries. If I failed to mention some names, I apologize for the oversight. The mind has a tendency to skip over some names when you're trying to recapture events, and people, from more than 50 years ago. To me, anybody who played in the Negro Leagues was a hero.

Some of the great players who came before my time, in the very early days of Negro Leagues baseball, I have omitted because I didn't see them play and I don't know anyone who did see them. I simply don't feel qualified to include them, but there is no doubt in my mind that many of them were good enough to be part of any all-time Negro Leagues team.

I'm sorry that I cannot include them and sorrier still that they never had the opportunity that I was fortunate enough, and young enough, to have.

—Monte Irvin

Catcher

Did **Josh Gibson** actually hit a ball clear out of Yankee Stadium? I heard that he did, but I don't know for sure because I didn't see it, and I don't know anyone who did.

Let me ask another question: did Babe Ruth actually point to the center-field seats in Wrigley Field in the 1932 World Series against the Cubs and then hit the ball right where he pointed?

That's what we have heard, but I don't know for sure that he did because I didn't see that either, and I don't know anyone who did. But from what we have all heard and read about the Babe, it's believable that he would have pointed to the seats and then hit the ball there.

The same goes for Josh Gibson. From what I have heard from old-time Negro Leagues players about his unbelievable power and from the shots I have seen him hit with my own eyes, I wouldn't doubt that he actually did hit a ball out of Yankee Stadium. He was capable of doing almost anything.

One player who swears he saw Gibson hit one clear out of Yankee Stadium is Jack Marshall of the Chicago American Giants. It happened in 1934, Marshall said.

"Gibson hit a ball off Slim Jones in a four-team doubleheader that we had in Yankee Stadium," said Marshall. "We had played the Black Yankees in the first game, and the Philadelphia Stars played the Pittsburgh Crawfords in the second game. They say a ball has never been hit out of Yankee Stadium. Well, that's a lie. Josh hit the ball over that triple deck next to the bullpen in left field. Over and out. I never will forget that, because we were getting ready to leave because we were going down to Hightstown, New Jersey, to play a night game, and we were standing in the aisle when that boy hit this ball."

The Sporting News credits Gibson with hitting a ball in Yankee Stadium that landed two feet from the top of the wall circling the bleachers in center field, some 580 feet from home plate. Estimates say that if the ball had been two feet higher, it would have sailed out of the Stadium and traveled about 700 feet.

Another account had Gibson hitting a ball that struck the rear wall of Yankee Stadium's left-field bullpen, about 500 feet from home plate.

Gibson had no peer for hitting home runs. In every league in which he ever played, he led in home runs and batting average. He had no weakness. He was big and strong—6'1", 215 pounds—bigger than Lou Gehrig and Jimmie Foxx and as big as Babe Ruth, and he was built like a tank. Derrick Brooks, a linebacker for the Tampa Bay Buccaneers, has a physique like Gibson's. Yes, Gibson was as strong as two men, could run like a deer, and had a great arm.

I've never seen anybody with a swing like Gibson's. He had very broad shoulders and great upper-body strength. He was unique. His swing was effortless. He would walk into the batter's box and turn his left sleeve up, and when he swung he lifted his left foot up just a little and put it right down, like Joe DiMaggio did. When he swung and missed, he wouldn't fall down, he'd follow through. Pitchers were afraid to throw him low and outside because that's the ball he would hit through the middle, and pitchers would be taking their life in their hands if they pitched him away. So they would pitch him inside.

If you want to compare Gibson to anyone, it would have to be Jimmie Foxx; both were strong right-handed hitters, were about the same size, were the same build, could run, and were easy to get along with. Gibson led the

Josh Gibson, one of the most powerful hitters the game has ever seen, makes a familiar trot around the bases.

Negro National League in home runs for 10 straight years, and records show he hit 75 homers in the 1931 season and 89 homers in another season, many of them against semipro teams.

We were playing against him in a little town near Pittsburgh, Monessen, Pennsylvania. It was a huge stadium, and Gibson hit a ball out of the park, across the street. The mayor of the town was at the game, and he said, "Stop the game and get that ball, because I have never seen anybody hit a ball that far." They said it traveled 575 feet. He was capable of doing anything.

And Josh had a perfect temperament. Everybody liked him. He got along with everybody. A great guy to be around, just a terrific person. He was good-natured, and he had a great sense of humor and would laugh at himself.

They used to call Gibson "the black Babe Ruth," and there was a sort of rivalry between them. Josh would stroll into the clubhouse and say, "Hey, tell me this, how many did the Babe, 'the King of Swat,' hit today?" Somebody would say, "He hit a couple," and Gibson would say, "Well, then maybe old Josh better get out and hit three."

There'll never be another man like him.

Gibson wasn't a Campanella as a catcher. He didn't like pop-ups. He could catch them, but he didn't like to. Campy would chase you away on pop-ups. Gibson was a little slow on pop fouls. He'd tell the third baseman and first baseman to take any foul pop his way, but that was the only thing he wasn't good at. He had a rifle for an arm. He could throw a strike to second base from his squat. And he could really run, especially for a big man.

But he was such a great hitter, and a great clutch-hitter. He would say, "Okay, you got me last time, you won't get me tonight," or "You need one run, I'll go up there and get it for you."

One time we were playing against him in Philadelphia, and our pitcher, Max Manning, struck him out twice with sidearm curveballs. During the ninth inning, with a couple of men on base, Manning threw that same pitch, and Josh hit it over the center-field fence. He was a right-handed hitter, but he could hit the ball as far to right field as a left-handed hitter could.

The great Walter Johnson once said, "There is a catcher that any big-league club would like to buy for $200,000. His name is Gibson. He can do everything. He hits the ball a mile. And he catches so easy he might as well be in a rocking chair. Throws like a rifle. Bill Dickey isn't as good a catcher. Too bad this Gibson is a colored fellow."

The tragedy of Josh Gibson is that he was born too soon. He was 34, and his best years behind him, when Jackie Robinson broke into organized baseball with Montreal. If Gibson had been 10 years younger—or if the color barrier had been broken 10 years earlier—I have no doubt that Josh would have been a major star in the big leagues, right up there with Mickey Cochrane, Gabby Hartnett, Bill Dickey, Yogi Berra, Roy Campanella, and Johnny Bench as the greatest catchers ever to play the game.

Sadly, Gibson suffered a stroke, and possibly a brain tumor, and he died a year later, three months before Robinson played his first game with the Dodgers in 1947.

If it were my choice, I would have made **Roy Campanella** the first African American to play in the major leagues. That's not to take anything away from Jackie Robinson. He did it and he was a success, but nobody knew at the time that he would become such a great player. If it had been me making the choice, I would have picked Campanella.

Campy was the best catcher in our league then; he was young, talented, humorous, and easy to get along with. I don't know this for a fact, but I have always suspected that if Branch Rickey was considering Campanella to break the color barrier, he might have rejected him because Campy's father was Italian and his mother black. It's possible that Rickey didn't want someone who was a product of a mixed marriage; he wanted a purebred, so to speak.

I first met Campanella when he was just a baby, 17 years old and playing for the Baltimore Elite Giants. He wasn't the roly-poly Campy that we knew when he played for the Dodgers, but he was chunky, and he always had a smile on his face. Even as a kid, he had such a good nature.

The first time I saw Campy was when Baltimore came to Newark. I had heard so much about him, so I went over to him before the game and said, "I understand you're the big deal down in Baltimore at the moment. I want you to know I rule this roost. Up here, I'm the main man."

"It's all right with me," he said. "I don't care. But you have to come to Baltimore."

Campy and I became great friends. In fact, for a long time, he was my best friend.

A few years later, I was invited to play for San Juan in the Puerto Rican Winter Leagues. Campy was also there, but he played for Caguas, a town about 40 miles away. I was in a terrible slump when Caguas came to San Juan, and Campy sought me out and said, "Dude"—Campy called everybody "Dude"; if he called you "Dude," that meant you were a good friend of his—he said, "Dude, I see you're not hitting much."

"I know," I said, "but I'm catching everything in center field, and I'm throwing out everybody that's running."

Roy Campanella challenged Josh Gibson as the premier catcher in the Negro Leagues and then went on to win three MVPs with the Dodgers.

"That's not enough, man," he said. "Here's what I'm going to do. If we get a lead, I'll give you the sign." Sure enough, the second time I came to bat we were down by about five runs. Campy got down to give the sign, and through his mask, so the umpire wouldn't hear, he whispered, "Fastball."

They threw me a fastball, and I took it.

Campy got in his crouch, and again, through his mask, he whispered, "Curveball."

I took that one, too, and Campy screamed, "Geez, what are you doing?"

"Let me tell you this, man," I said. "You don't have the best reputation for telling the truth. I had to check you out."

On the next pitch, he again whispered what was coming. This time I believed him, and I hit a home run.

A month later, we played Caguas again, and Campy was in a slump. I said, "You did me a favor; I'm going to do you a favor in return."

Campanella, who was married, had brought his wife and two kids with him to Puerto Rico. So I told him, "You need to get away from your wife and two kids for a night just to clear your head. Come on over to San Juan and we'll go out and do a little dancing or something. Get away from it. Relax yourself."

Campy got a driver to take him to San Juan, and I took him to a night-club. He was dancing and having a good time. At the time, he drank only Coca-Cola. I figured he needed to loosen up a little, so I ordered him a Coke and when he wasn't looking, I poured a little rum into the Coke. After about an hour, he said, "You know, dude, I don't know why I feel so good."

"See," I said. "I told you. Get away from those kids for a night and you'll relax. You just needed a little freedom to clear your head."

It was nearly 2:00 AM, closing time at the club, and Campy's driver wanted to get home. Campy told me he was going to leave. "Dude, I know what you have been doing," he said. "I'm not dumb. But let me tell you what. In about a month, invite me back and do the same thing all over again."

The kicker to the story is that many years later, shortly before he died, Campy's wife told me, "You taught my husband to drink rum and Coke, and he's still drinking it."

Another time, I was playing in Mexico City and Campy was there, too, playing in Monterey, about 500 miles north. It was the last game of the season, and we were playing against Monterey in Mexico City. Monterey had a pitcher named Lazaro Salazar, a Cuban left-hander: a good pitcher and a good hitter. They had us beat, 2–1, in the bottom of the ninth.

Jorge Pasquel, the father of Mexican baseball, was sitting in the box seats, right behind home plate. With two outs and nobody on, Ray Dandridge singled, and I was coming up with the tying run on first base. I was in the batting circle, and when Dandridge got his base hit, Pasquel yelled at me, "Hey, Monte, come here."

"Jorge," I said, "I'm getting ready to hit."

"Never mind," he said. "Come here."

I went to the box where Pasquel was sitting, and he put his arms around me and said, "You hit a home run for me."

"Jorge," I said, "do you see how hard Salazar is throwing?"

"No, never mind," he said. "You hit a home run for me, for your friend, for Jorge."

"I'll do the best I can, Jorge, but I can't promise a home run," I said. "I'll try to keep the rally going."

"No, no," he insisted. "Never mind that, you hit a home run for me."

At that time, I always used to take one pitch because very rarely would I swing at a ball and miss it. Taking one pitch was no big deal. Salazar's first pitch was a fastball right over the outside corner. I took it. Strike one. The next pitch was a sharp breaking curveball. I swung and fouled it over the grandstand.

The count was 0–2, and something said to me, "Be ready now because Campy is going to want to strike me out with three pitches." I guessed fastball and hit it over the center-field fence for a home run. We won the game, 3–2.

By the time I circled the bases and got to home plate, Jorge Pasquel had climbed out of his box seat and was standing at home plate waiting to greet me. He shook my hand, and in his hand was $500.

Campy hadn't left the field. He was still standing at home plate, also waiting for me.

"Geez," he said, "you're the luckiest son of a so-and-so."

He was ranting and raving about how lucky I was.

"Settle down," I said. "Jorge just gave me $500 and told me to give you $250 for calling the right pitch."

A big smile spread across Campy's face. "You my main man," he said.

Even when he was young, Campanella was a good hitter, a pull hitter. He would pull almost every pitch. In order to get him out, we tried to crowd him inside and then throw him change-ups away.

Campy went on to play nine years with Baltimore. Eventually, he challenged Josh Gibson as the premier catcher in the Negro National League.

In Baltimore there was a young fellow named Ziggy Marcelle whose father, Oliver, had been a great Negro Leagues third baseman in the early days, before I got into the league. One day Ziggy went to Biz Mackey, the manager of the Elite Giants, and said, "Skip, I'd like to try out."

"What position do you play?" Mackey asked.

"I'm a catcher," Ziggy said.

"We have a catcher, Roy Campanella," Mackey said.

"Yeah, I know," Ziggy said, "but you can use two catchers, give Campy some relief once in a while."

Mackey said, "Okay, if we get a lead, I'll put you in and see what you can do."

Ziggy waited for his chance, but it was a close game and Mackey kept Campanella in the whole way, and Campy hit two home runs, threw out a base runner, and blocked the plate and tagged out a base runner trying to score. When the game was over, Ziggy went to Mackey and said, "I just want you to know, I play other positions."

In 1946, when Branch Rickey signed Jackie Robinson, he also signed four other players from the Negro Leagues, including Campy and Don Newcombe, and he never gave the Negro Leagues teams any money—not a penny.

Campanella was 25 years old, and he was ready for the major leagues, but the major leagues weren't ready for him. Robinson went to Montreal, the Dodgers' top farm team in the Triple A International League; Campanella and Newcombe went to Nashua, New Hampshire, in the Class B Eastern League. Campy overmatched the league and was named Most Valuable Player.

At Nashua his manager was Walter Alston, who would be Campy's manager with the Dodgers in a few years. Alston had so much respect for Campanella's knowledge of the game that once, when Walter was ejected, he turned the lineup card over to Roy and made him manager for a day, so you could say that Campanella was the first black manager in professional baseball. Nashua won the game, and Campy retired undefeated as a manager.

The following year, when Robinson broke in with the Dodgers, Campanella moved up to Montreal and again was named the league's Most Valuable Player. Paul Richards, managing in Buffalo, called him "the best catcher in the business, major or minor leagues."

By then Campy was a finished product as a catcher. He didn't need seasoning in the minor leagues. He had honed his skills during his nine years playing in the Negro Leagues. When he got to Brooklyn, he would often catch both ends of a doubleheader in sweltering heat and humidity. When he was asked about it, Campanella said, "Hell, doubleheaders are nothing. In the Negro Leagues I used to catch four games in one day."

Preacher Roe was a savvy, veteran left-hander for the Dodgers in the 1950s, a guy who knew all the tricks of the trade, within and outside of the rules, and used every one of them. Roe admitted in an article in *Sports Illustrated* that one of his main weapons was the spitball, which was banned by baseball and is a pitch that darts and dives unpredictably, making it as difficult to catch as it is to hit. Campanella had no trouble handling Roe's wet one.

"I caught spitters in the Negro Leagues for years," Campy explained.

Campanella's stay in the minor leagues was more for social reasons than seasoning, however. In 1948 Rickey sent him to St. Paul, choosing Roy as the player to integrate the American Association. By May Campy was batting .325, with 13 homers and 39 RBIs in 35 games, and the Dodgers brought him to Brooklyn, where he soon supplanted Bruce Edwards as the Dodgers' number one catcher.

It wasn't long before Campanella was a star in the National League. In 10 seasons he batted over .300 three times, drove in more than 100 runs three times, and hit more than 40 home runs once and more than 30 four times. People used to say that he did so well because he hit in Ebbets Field, a bandbox. That's true, he did hit in Ebbets Field, but so did everybody else.

By the time Campanella became established in Brooklyn, the wraps were off Robinson, and people found that he had a tendency to be abrasive, quite different from Campanella, who was friendly, good-natured, and outgoing—a delightful guy to be around. Everybody liked him. He didn't have any enemies, but he and Jackie occasionally had their differences.

One time Jackie called Campy an Uncle Tom, and Campy let him have it. He said, "Jackie, let me tell you something. My name is damn near as big as yours. I don't have any hang-up on race. All I want to do is play good baseball and set an example for those who come after me. Don't you try to tell me what to do. I'll do what I want to do."

As a result, he and Jackie stopped speaking for a while.

Because catcher is such a tough position and Campy was often getting hurt, he never put two great years back-to-back, but he won three Most Valuable Player awards, and he did it in alternate years—in 1951, when he batted .325, hit 33 homers, and drove in 108; in 1953, when he batted .312, hit 41 homers, and led the league with 142 RBIs; and in 1955, when he batted .318, hit 32 homers, and drove in 107.

He was something. As a catcher, he had no peer. He was quick as a cat behind the plate, was great on pop-ups, had a great arm, had a quick release, blocked balls in the dirt, and was intelligent. He called a great game. He knew how to set up hitters. He was a terrific catcher. Campy, Yogi Berra, and Johnny Bench—what can you say about those guys? How can you get any better than they were?

I have always said that we—the New York Giants, that is—got lucky, because in the 1951 playoff Campy was injured and didn't play the second and third games. If he had, it might have been a different story. Not only did the Dodgers miss his bat, but they also missed his intelligence behind the plate. I'm not taking anything away from Rube Walker, who was a very competent catcher, but he had come to the Dodgers from the Cubs in midseason, and he caught only 23 games for the Dodgers. Campy was more familiar with the Dodgers' pitchers.

When Ralph Branca came in to pitch to Bobby Thomson in the ninth inning of the third playoff game, his first pitch was a fastball right down the middle. Bobby took it for strike one. Branca came back with the same pitch, and Bobby hit it out to win the game and the pennant. Somehow I doubt that Campy would have called the same pitch, and who knows what would have happened then.

As great a career as Campanella had with the Dodgers—good enough for election to the Hall of Fame—it might have been even better if he had gotten his chance to play in the major leagues earlier than 1948, and if he hadn't had that terrible automobile accident that left him confined to a wheelchair for the rest of his life.

It happened in the winter between the 1957 season, the Dodgers' last in Brooklyn, and the 1958 season, their first in Los Angeles. Campy was only 36. He probably had some productive years left.

The day I learned of Campy's accident was one of the saddest of my life. You say to yourself, if bad things have to happen to people, why did it have to happen to a great guy like Roy Campanella?

Some historians say that the greatest catcher in Negro Leagues baseball was not Josh Gibson or Roy Campanella; it was James Raleigh "Biz" Mackey, who caught until he was 50. In 1954 the *Pittsburgh Courier* conducted a poll to choose the all-time Negro Leagues team, and **Biz Mackey** was selected as the number one catcher.

I can't pick Mackey over Gibson and Campanella because by the time I saw Biz he was in his forties and at the end of his career. But from what I saw of him at that age, I couldn't argue with those who think he was the best.

Mackey was my manager with the Newark Eagles for a few years, and I probably learned more baseball from him than from anybody else I've ever been around. He was such a great teacher. He and Campanella were teammates with the Baltimore Elite Giants, and Campy told me Biz taught him everything he knew about catching. Campy called Mackey "the master of defense of all catchers."

Biz was a master at setting up hitters, and he was known for throwing runners out at second base from a squatting position. He was just a great, great catcher and a switch-hitter with good power from both sides of the plate. Mostly he was a line-drive hitter who batted .423 with 20 home runs and a .698 slugging percentage for the Hilldale Daisies in the Eastern Colored League in 1923. Two years later he batted .375 to help Hilldale beat the Kansas City Monarchs in the Negro Leagues World Series.

One time when Mackey was managing the Eagles, we had an important game against the Baltimore Elite Giants. Biz was 45 years old at the time, but he told our pitcher, Max Manning, "I'm catching tonight. Just work with me. Don't shake me off."

Manning pitched a 5–0 shutout. I was playing center field, and I could see how Mackey was working the hitters. He truly was a master—and a great guy, to boot. On long bus rides, I would sit with Mackey, and I would ask him about all the Negro Leagues stars he played with that I didn't see. Most of what I know about those old Negro Leagues players, such as Rap Dixon, John Beckwith, and Slim Jones, I learned from Mackey, who was a great storyteller.

Biz Mackey caught until he was 50 years old, and those who saw him in his prime—unfortunately, I did not—rate him higher than both Gibson and Campanella.

Something not many people know about Mackey is that he headed up a team of Negro Leagues All-Stars that was invited to go to Japan in 1927. They were the first American professional team to play in Japan, seven years before Babe Ruth and Connie Mack took a team of major league All-Stars there.

One time at a speaking engagement I had a question-and-answer session after my talk, and people were asking me about the great Negro Leagues stars of the past. Red Smith, the highly respected New York sportswriter, was there, and he said, "Monte, I have heard you talking about some of those old-timers. Why is it that you haven't mentioned **Louis Santop**?"

"Red," I said, "the reason I haven't mentioned him is that I didn't think there was anybody here who knew anything about him."

At 6'4" and 240 pounds, Louis Santop struck an imposing figure and was known for his tape-measure home runs.

"Well, I did," said Red, who started his career in Philadelphia and saw Santop play for the Philadelphia Giants. "When he passed away, I got on a train, and I went to Philadelphia for his funeral, because I had seen him play and I knew what he could do."

"I never saw him play," I said, "but I heard about him from Biz Mackey, and Biz said he was awesome."

Santop was a big guy, 6'4", 240 pounds, and a left-handed power hitter who was known for his tape-measure home runs. They say that in one game in 1912, during the so-called dead-ball era, he hit a ball 500 feet. Playing for the New York Lincoln Giants from 1911 to 1914, he had batting averages of .470, .422, .429, and .455.

Santop switched to the Hilldale Daisies in 1917, spent two years in the army during World War I, and when he returned he was such a great drawing card, he was paid $500 per month, a king's ransom in those days.

After he retired as a player, Santop went into broadcasting and ended his days tending bar in Philadelphia.

I never saw Louis Santop, and I didn't see Biz Mackey in his prime, but except for Josh Gibson and Roy Campanella, I didn't see a better catcher in the Negro Leagues than **Elston Howard**.

Ellie, a four-sport star in a St. Louis high school, figured the Cardinals would sign him after he had spent four days in their tryout camp. He was so sure the Cards would sign him, Ellie turned down scholarship offers from Big Ten schools who wanted him for baseball and football. But the Cardinals never made him an offer, so Ellie signed with the Kansas City Monarchs.

He was in his third season with the Monarchs when he was sold to the Yankees in July 1950 and broke in with Muskegon (Michigan) in the Class A Central League. Ellie batted .283 for Muskegon with nine homers and 42 RBIs in 54 games and then went off to spend two years in the army.

When he returned, Howard was assigned to Kansas City in the Triple A American Association, batting .286 in 1953. The following year he went to Toronto in the Triple A International League and had a breakout year, a .330 average, 22 homers, and 109 RBIs. He was named the league's Most Valuable Player.

That earned him a chance to go to spring training with the Yankees in 1955, and when he made the team, he became the first African American to play for the Yankees, eight years after Jackie Robinson broke the color barrier. Shamefully, the Yankees, the most prestigious team in sports, was among the last major league teams to integrate. They had signed Puerto Rico–born Vic Power before they signed Howard, and Power rose through their farm system quickly and appeared to be on a fast track to the Bronx. But the controversial Power was "not the Yankees type," whatever that is, and he was traded to the Athletics.

Elston Howard apparently was the Yankees type: quiet, unassuming, well-bred, intelligent, a gentleman, and extremely likable. He soon became a favorite of Yankees fans and his teammates. But Ellie had another problem: when he joined the Yankees, he was blocked by a Hall of Famer, one of the most popular Yankees ever, Yogi Berra, who had won his second Most Valuable Player award and would win his third the year Howard arrived.

Elston Howard began his career with the Kansas City Monarchs and was purchased by the Yankees in 1950, becoming the first black player to wear the famous pinstripes five years later.

Howard had to wait his turn to move into his best position, catcher. In his rookie season, he caught only nine games and played 75 in the outfield, batting .290 with 10 homers and 43 RBIs. Each year Howard got more games behind the plate, but it wasn't until 1960 that he would replace Berra as the team's number one catcher.

The Yankees said they were waiting for the right man. You'd have to say they couldn't have done better than Elston Howard."—Norm Siebern

Once he got his chance, Howard became a star. He made the All-Star team nine times, was named American League Most Valuable Player in 1963, and was a mainstay on Yankees teams that won nine pennants and four World Series.

Although the Yankees waited a long time to get a black player, when they got one, they certainly made the right choice. I loved Ellie. I thought he was a great man. As Norm Siebern said, "The Yankees said they were waiting for the right man. You'd have to say they couldn't have done better than Elston Howard."

The Negro Leagues had so many outstanding catchers, I may have done an injustice to some guys by leaving them off my list.

No discussion of Negro Leagues catchers would be complete without mention of Larry Brown and Egghead Clarke, whose real first name was Robert. Brown played for and managed several teams, but his primary team was the Memphis Red Sox. He was a light hitter, but as a catcher he was classy. He did everything on his toes

Clarke was similar to Brown, also a light hitter but an excellent catcher, mainly for the Baltimore Black Sox and the Baltimore Elite Giants. He called a good game and worked well with pitchers. He was great at setting up a hitter, and he was especially good at foul pops—so good, in fact, that people would come to the games early just to watch Egghead catch foul pops in practice.

Some Negro Leagues catchers I never saw play and don't feel qualified to judge, and others fall just below my top five, but based on what I have read and heard about some and my personal observation of others, these catchers are also worthy of mention: Bruce Petway, Buck Ewing, Chappie Johnson, Quincy Trouppe, Frank Duncan, Sam Hairston, Otha Bailey, and Ray Noble.

17

Career Summaries

Catcher	Years	Teams
Josh Gibson *Batted .483 (14–29) in nine East-West All-Star Games*	1928–46	Homestead Grays, Pittsburgh Crawfords
Roy Campanella *Played in the Mexican League in 1943, leading loop in runs scored with 74*	1937–42, 1944–45	Baltimore Elite Giants
Biz Mackey *Batted over .400 three times*	1918–47	San Antonio Giants, Indianapolis ABCs, Hilldale Daisies, Philadelphia Stars, Washington/Baltimore Elite Giants, Newark Eagles, Newark Dodgers, Nashville Giants
Louis Santop *Batted .333 for Hilldale in 1924 World Series*	1909–26	Fort Worth Wonders, Oklahoma Monarchs, Philadelphia Giants, Lincoln Giants, Chicago American Giants, Lincoln Stars, Brooklyn Royal Giants, Hilldale Daisies
Elston Howard *Drove in 43 runs in 48 games in 1950*	1948–50	Kansas City Monarchs

TWO

First Baseman

If I had to choose between **Buck Leonard** and Lou Gehrig, I'm not too sure I wouldn't pick Buck Leonard.

I know that's saying a lot. I saw Gehrig play when I was a kid, and I know the kind of player he was, but I also saw Leonard and played against him. He was terrific: a great fielder and a great hitter, a left-handed power hitter and a high-average hitter like Gehrig. Buck was a dead pull hitter. You could shoot it out of a cannon and he'd pull it.

Defensively, because of his smoothness around the bag, the major leaguer Leonard was most often compared with was George Sisler. Eddie Gottlieb, who was a booking agent for Negro Leagues teams and later became president of the Philadelphia team in the National Basketball Association, called Leonard "as smooth a first baseman as I ever saw."

1. BUCK LEONARD

2. GEORGE GILES

3. MULE SUTTLES

4. LUKE EASTER

5. BOB BOYD

Buck played with the Homestead Grays for 17 years, the longest term of service with one team in Negro Leagues history, and teamed with Josh Gibson (Gibson batting third, Leonard fourth) to help the Grays win nine straight Negro National League titles, from 1937 to 1945, and to form what I believe to be one of the most awesome one-two batting punches in baseball history.

At a time when it was common for a first baseman in the Negro Leagues to play the role of clown and entertain the crowd with his antics, Leonard never went in for that stuff. He was all baseball. In those days, the average salary in the Negro Leagues was $200 per month, but Buck was such a valued member of the Grays that he got to the point where they were paying him $1,000 per month and $2 per day for meal money, making him the third-highest-paid player in Negro Leagues baseball, behind Satchel Paige and Gibson.

Leonard didn't hit the ball as far as Gibson did—Buck was more of a line-drive hitter—but he was just as lethal as Josh. When you played the Homestead Grays and you had to face these guys back-to-back, if you could get by them, get them out three or four times, that was a major accomplishment. If one didn't get you, the other one would. Gibson was called "the black Babe Ruth" and Leonard "the black Lou Gehrig"; the comparisons to those legendary Yankees are not far-fetched. In my view, you can put Leonard and Gibson right up there with the greatest slugging tandems in baseball history, with Ruth and Gehrig, Ted Williams and Jimmie Foxx, Hank Aaron and Eddie Mathews, Roger Maris and Mickey Mantle, Willie Mays and Willie McCovey, Jose Canseco and Mark McGwire, and David Ortiz and Manny Ramirez.

Leonard was a phenomenon, playing professionally until he was 48 years old. That was in 1955 when Buck played in 62 games for Durango in the Mexican League, batting .312 with 13 homers.

A little-known fact is that Gibson and Leonard almost became the first African Americans to play in the major leagues. The Homestead Grays had moved to Washington, D.C., in 1937, playing some home games in Griffith Stadium when the Senators were on the road.

Clark Griffith, the Senators owner, could sit in his office and look out through a window and see the field. He watched Josh and Buck hit tape-measure home runs and fantasized about them wearing the uniform of his Senators and what they could do to improve his team. Griffith was certain those two players alone would transform his perennial cellar dwellers into contenders in the American League, and he was tempted to sign them for Washington, 10 years before Robinson joined the Dodgers. In the end, Griffith admitted he didn't have the courage to be the owner to break the color line, and Gibson and Leonard's chance passed them by.

Buck Leonard was with the Homestead Grays for 17 years, the longest term of service with one team in Negro Leagues history.

What a pity Leonard never got to show what he could do in his prime and that fans of major league baseball never got to see the kind of player he was. In the Negro National League, he made the All-Star team 12 times, had a career batting average of .341, won three batting titles, and averaged 34 home runs per season from 1936 to 1943. But by the time Robinson broke in, Leonard, then 39, was considered too old to be the first.

In 1951 Bill Veeck offered Leonard a contract to play for the St. Louis Browns, but Buck, knowing his best days were behind him, turned down Veeck's offer. He said he didn't want to embarrass anyone or hurt the chances of African American players who would come later. He was 43 at the time.

"I only wish I could have played in the big leagues when I was young enough to show what I could do," he said. "When an offer was given me to join up, I was too old and I knew it."

Leonard did get a chance to play in organized baseball, but only briefly, and in the minor leagues. In his midforties, he played 10 games for Portsmouth (Virginia), where he got his start in Negro Leagues baseball at the age of 16. In those 10 games, Buck batted .333.

Not only was Buck Leonard the greatest first baseman in Negro Leagues history, he was also clearly one of its greatest players. As testimony to that, after Satchel Paige became the first Negro Leagues player elected to the Hall of Fame in Cooperstown in 1971, a year later Leonard and Josh Gibson were the second and third elected.

When his playing career was over, Buck stayed involved with baseball by helping to form the Rocky Mount, North Carolina, team in the Class A Carolina League and serving as the club's vice president. He also worked as a probation officer, was athletics director of the Rocky Mount school district, and operated a thriving real estate business in Rocky Mount, the city of his birth.

Buck never received a high school diploma when he was young, because Rocky Mount did not have integrated schools. He took a high school equivalency course and got his diploma at the age of 52.

22

George Giles is a name you rarely hear mentioned when people talk about the greatest players in Negro Leagues history, but let me tell you, George belongs right up there with the best of them.

I saw Giles play with the Lincoln Giants and the New York Black Yankees. He was a great first baseman. He didn't hit like Buck Leonard did, but he could field. He is considered the best defensive first baseman ever to play in the Negro Leagues. "Double Duty" Radcliffe called Giles the best first baseman he ever saw.

George Giles is considered the best defensive first baseman ever to play in the Negro Leagues.

In his time, it was said that, except for Cool Papa Bell, Giles was the fastest runner in baseball. He wasn't a big power guy, more a line-drive hitter who choked up on the bat and slapped the ball around, a great contact hitter who was tough to strike out and could run like a deer. With his speed and batting left-handed, he got a lot of infield hits and beat out a lot of bunts, and he had a lifetime batting average of .300.

From 1929 to 1931, Giles was a key member of the St. Louis Stars, one of the best Negro Leagues teams. In one eight-game series against major leaguers, the Stars won six games. Giles ended his career playing for the Satchel Paige All-Stars in 1939.

Giles retired in 1939 and, for a time, managed a hotel in Kansas.

Although he never got the chance to play in the major leagues, he lived to see his grandson make it. Brian Giles, a second baseman, spent six seasons in the major leagues with the Mets, Brewers, White Sox, and Mariners in the 1980s and 1990s.

George Giles, who played with the Lincoln Giants and New York Black Yankees, was considered the best-fielding first baseman and one of the fastest players in Negro Leagues history.

*T*he first family of Negro Leagues baseball was the Taylor family—Charles Isam (known as C.I.), James (known as "Candy" Jim), John (known as "Steel Arm" Johnny), and Benjamin Harrison (known as Ben)—four brothers whose combined experience in the Negro Leagues totaled more than 100 years. Three of the brothers ("Candy" Jim, "Steel Arm" Johnny, and Ben) were players; three (C.I., "Candy" Jim, and Ben) were managers.

Benjamin Harrison Taylor's career spanned 28 years as an elite player with, among others, the Indianapolis ABCs, Birmingham Giants, Lincoln Giants, and Chicago American Giants. The youngest of the four brothers, Ben Taylor was also a highly regarded manager and teacher with the Indianapolis ABCs, New York Cubans, Bacharach Giants, and Brooklyn Eagles. He was an umpire, too.

As a fielder, Taylor was in a class by himself, especially adept at digging throws out of the dirt. As a hitter, Taylor is the only Negro Leagues first baseman mentioned on a par with Buck Leonard. Like Leonard, Taylor was a lethal left-handed hitter, and, in fact, Leonard credits Taylor with helping him to hone his abundant skills.

"I got most of my learning from Ben Taylor," Buck once said. "He helped me when I first broke in with his team [the Baltimore Stars in 1933]. He had been the best first baseman in Negro Leagues baseball up until that time, and he was the one who really taught me to play first base."

Although not the power threat that Leonard was, Taylor was a devastating line-drive hitter who anchored the Indianapolis ABCs lineup in the 1920s as their cleanup batter. It was in that role that he picked up the nickname "Old Reliable," a quarter of a century before the Yankees' Tommy Henrich was given the same sobriquet. In the first three seasons of the 1920s, Taylor strung together averages of .323, .407, and .358.

Ben Taylor finally got his long overdue reward when he was elected to the Baseball Hall of Fame in 2006, 53 years after his death.

I played with George "Mule" Suttles on the Newark Eagles. He started his career—and he played for 25 years—as an outfielder, and then when he got a little older and heavier, he moved to first base. Before I got there, **Mule Suttles** was part of the Eagles' famed Million Dollar Infield, Mule at first base, Dick Seay at second base, Willie Wells at shortstop, and Ray Dandridge at third base.

Suttles was a good hitter, a power hitter, whose best years were with the St. Louis Stars from 1926 to 1930. In that time, he led the league in home runs twice and in batting average, doubles, and triples once each. Mule is one of only seven Negro Leagues players on record as having hit for the cycle—a single, double, triple, and home run in one game—a feat he accomplished on May 15, 1926.

Until Josh Gibson came along, Suttles was the Negro Leagues' top right-handed power hitter. He didn't hit for a consistently high average, and he wasn't much of a fielder, either in the outfield or at first base, but he could hit a baseball a long way.

Mule Suttles was said to have used a 50-ounce bat and to have handled it like a toothpick.

25

Mule was a monster of a man, 6'6", about 250 pounds, and they say he used a 50-ounce bat and handled it like a toothpick. I heard so many stories of Suttles's power from people like Willie Wells, who played with him in Newark and Cuba, and Charlie Gehringer, who told me, "He could hit a ball nine miles."

They say Suttles once hit three home runs in one inning against the Memphis Red Sox. Another story I heard is that when he was a player, Leo Durocher was playing in an exhibition game against Mule, who had a single, double, and triple in his first three times at bat. When he came up a fourth time, the pitcher, Jim Weaver, who was with the Cubs, asked Leo how to pitch to Mule.

"Just throw the ball and pray," Durocher said.

I was in Cuba a few years ago, and they're still talking about a ball Suttles hit down there. I asked one old-time Cuban sportswriter about it, and he said it was the longest home run ever hit in Cuba. It was measured at 598 feet.

Suttles was the best curveball hitter I've ever seen. If you got him out, you had to get him out on fastballs. Don't throw him a curveball. He was deadly hitting a curveball. Mule seemed to save his best games for the big stage. In five All-Star Games, he batted .412 with a slugging percentage of .833, two home runs, and six RBIs. His 1933 home run was the first one ever hit in an All-Star Game. His second came off the great Martin Dihigo in the bottom of the eleventh inning with two outs, two runners on base, and the score tied, 8–8, in the 1935 All-Star Game.

In 1929, playing against a team of major leaguers, Mule proved he could hit major league pitching by belting five home runs in 26 games and batting close to .400.

By doing exhaustive research, statisticians discovered that in 77 at-bats in barnstorming games against major leaguers, Mule hit 11 home runs, which would compute to more than 80 homers in a 154-game season.

Another guy whose best years were spent in the Negro Leagues was Luscious "Luke" Easter, but at least he got his chance to play in the major leagues. **Luke Easter** was playing with the Homestead Grays when the Cleveland Indians signed him prior to the 1949 season and started him out with San Diego in the Pacific Coast League. In August he was promoted to the majors to become the third African American, after Larry Doby and Satchel Paige, to play for the Indians.

Luke Easter was acquired by the Indians in 1949, ending his Negro Leagues career, and he is believed to have hit the longest home run at Cleveland's Municipal Stadium.

So impressed were the Indians with Easter's power that in June of the following year they traded Mickey Vernon, who had won the American League batting championship with the Indians in 1946, in order to open up first base for Luke. Easter responded with a .280 average, 28 home runs, and 107 RBIs in his rookie season. In his first three years in Cleveland, Luke averaged 29 home runs and 102 runs batted in and was one of the most fearsome sluggers in the American League.

An imposing figure at 6'5" and 240 pounds, Luke wowed fans, teammates, and opponents with his awesome power, the kind he had displayed in the Negro Leagues. He once hit a home run into the center-field seats in the Polo Grounds, some 480 feet away, something that only Henry Aaron, Joe Adcock, and Lou Brock ever did. In Cleveland he hit what was believed to be the longest shot ever in Municipal Stadium, a blast into the upper right-field stands on June 27, 1950, that was estimated at 477 feet.

One time a fan told Easter that he had seen Luke's longest home run, to which Luke replied, "If it came down, it wasn't my longest."

When the Indians released him in May 1954, Easter returned to the minor leagues and spent eight years with Buffalo and Rochester of the International League, playing well into his forties. In Rochester he was a huge fan favorite, one of the most popular players in Red Wings history. He refused to leave the ballpark until every fan who requested an autograph was satisfied.

Luke was a friendly and likable character and something of an enigma. At various times, he said he was born in St. Louis, Missouri, and Jonestown, Mississippi, either in 1911, 1914, 1915, or 1921, which meant in his rookie season with the Indians, he was either 38, 35, 34, or—the least believable—28 years old.

Like Babe Ruth, Easter not only hit tape-measure home runs, but he also had difficulty remembering names, and he called everybody "Bub."

When Luke finally retired from baseball in 1963, he was either 52, or 49, or 48, or—the least believable—42 years old.

Sadly, Luke met a tragic end in 1979. Having returned to his former home-town of Cleveland, he became the chief union steward for the Aircraft Workers Alliance. On March 29, 1979, Easter drove to a bank in nearby Euclid to deposit $40,000 in union funds. He was accosted in the bank parking lot by two men carrying shotguns who ordered him to hand over the money. When Luke resisted, one of the robbers fired a shotgun blast in his chest, killing the big man instantly.

They called **Bob Boyd** "the Rope," because of the line drives he hit. Bob was a good hitter—not in a class with Buck Leonard and some of those other guys, but a good hitter, an outstanding fielder (he made only 38 errors in 4,029 chances in the major leagues)—and he could run.

Bob was something of a pioneer. After playing three seasons in the Negro American League with the Memphis Red Sox, batting .352, .369, and .371, he signed with the Chicago White Sox and, as a 31-year-old rookie, was the first African American to play for them. Later he was drafted by the Orioles and became their first regular player to hit over .300 after the Orioles moved from St. Louis to Baltimore, batting .318 in 1957. That placed him fourth in the American League, behind Ted Williams, Mickey Mantle, and Gene Woodling and ahead of Nellie Fox, Minnie Minoso, Bill Skowron, and Roy Sievers, which I would say is pretty good company.

Bob Boyd was nicknamed "the Rope" for his propensity to hit hard line drives in the Negro Leagues and the majors.

29

Boyd batted .309 the following year, and the year after that, playing for the Orioles against the Washington Senators, he started a triple play on Opening Day.

Boyd spent nine seasons in the big leagues with four teams: the White Sox, Orioles, Athletics, and Braves.

Three other first basemen I should mention are Ben Taylor, James "Red" Moore, and Jim West.

Taylor was the youngest of the four Taylor brothers (C.I., "Steel Arm" Johnny, and "Candy" Jim were the others) and the mentor of Buck Leonard. Taylor was managing the Baltimore Stars when Leonard joined them in 1933. Ben was considered to be the finest first baseman in the Negro Leagues, and he tutored Leonard so well that Buck eventually replaced him as the Negro Leagues' top first baseman.

I broke in with the Newark Eagles with Red Moore, who was as flashy a fielding first baseman as I've ever seen. I'd compare him with Vic Power for flashiness. He was so good at scooping throws out of the dirt that somebody once called him "the greatest retriever of scattergun throws in America." Red liked to put on a show around the bag, and people used to arrive at the ballpark early just to watch him take infield practice—that's how much of a fancy Dan he was at first base.

Although he was a good left-handed hitter, unfortunately Red was more of a line-drive hitter and not in a class with guys like Buck Leonard, Luke Easter, and Mule Suttles as a power hitter. Most teams want their first basemen to be big boppers, so the Eagles eventually moved Mule Suttles from the outfield to first base, and even though we sacrificed something on defense, Suttles's booming bat was a great asset to our offense. Moore moved on to play with the Atlanta Black Crackers and the Baltimore Elite Giants.

West, whose primary team was the Philadelphia Stars, was very similar to Moore: a fancy fielder but a light hitter, except for one thing. For some reason—and nobody has ever been able to explain it or understand it—West could hit Satchel Paige better than anybody I've ever seen.

Other Negro Leagues first basemen worthy of note are Lyman Bostock Sr. and Len Pearson, my teammate with the Newark Eagles who started as an outfielder and then moved to first base and became a very good first baseman. He was one of the best athletes I've ever seen. In football he could throw the ball 70 yards and kick it 65 yards. Also noteworthy are George Alt-man, George Crowe, Showboat Thomas, Popsicle Harris, Ted Strong, Jelly Taylor, Archie Ware, Buck O'Neil, and even Oscar Charleston, who moved to first base from the outfield late in his career.

It may seem that first base was a lean position in the Negro Leagues, and that's probably the case, for two reasons. For one, the first baseman often was more of a clown than a ballplayer, a guy whose job was to entertain fans with his antics. (That explains why Goose Tatum, the famous Harlem Globetrot-ter clown, made the West All-Star team in 1947.) Another reason the posi-tion seems lean is because Buck Leonard was so great that he overshadowed every other first baseman.

Career Summaries

First Baseman	Years	Teams
Buck Leonard *Hit a record three home runs in 11 East-West All-Star Games*	1933–50	Baltimore Stars, Brooklyn Royal Giants, Homestead Grays
George Giles *Played for three teams (Monarchs, Wolves, and Grays) in 1933*	1927–38	Kansas City Monarchs, St. Louis Stars, Brooklyn Eagles, New York Black Yankees, Philadelphia Stars, Detroit Wolves, Homestead Grays, Pittsburgh Crawfords, Baltimore Black Sox
Mule Suttles *Had .882 East-West All-Star Game slugging percentage, 72 points higher than anyone else's*	1918–44	Birmingham Black Barons, St. Louis Stars, Baltimore Black Sox, Detroit Wolves, Washington Pilots, Chicago American Giants, Newark Eagles, New York Black Yankees
Luke Easter *Hit .336 in his two Negro Leagues seasons*	1946–48	Homestead Grays
Bob Boyd *Batted over .300 in each of his four seasons in the Negro Leagues*	1947–50	Memphis Red Sox

THREE

Second Baseman

Baseball's emancipation proclamation went into effect on April 15, 1947, when **Jackie Robinson** made his major league debut with the Brooklyn Dodgers at Ebbets Field, playing first base and batting second against the Boston Braves.

At long last the doors to the major leagues were opened for African Americans, as well as dark-skinned Cubans, Puerto Ricans, Mexicans, Dominicans, Panamanians, Venezuelans, Bahamians, and Virgin Islanders.

It's well known that Robinson had been summoned to the Dodgers' offices in Brooklyn on the pretense that Branch Rickey wanted to talk to him about joining a Negro Leagues team that Rickey was planning to put in Brooklyn. After a while it became apparent that Rickey's actual intention was to discover if Jackie was the right man to break baseball's longtime color barrier.

During the course of a lengthy interview, Rickey pulled no punches. He played devil's advocate, acting the part of a merciless bigot, all the while

1. JACKIE ROBINSON

2. SAMMY T. HUGHES

3. NEWT ALLEN

4. JIM GILLIAM

5. PIPER DAVIS

Jackie Robinson (batting) played only a few months in the Negro Leagues before breaking the color barrier in the majors and embarking on his groundbreaking, courageous Hall of Fame career.

trying to give Jackie an idea of what he would face from fans, opponents, and even his own teammates in organized baseball.

At one point, Robinson said, "Mr. Rickey, do you want a man who is afraid to fight back?"

"Jackie," Rickey bellowed in reply, "I want a man with guts enough *not* to fight back."

The selection of Robinson to be the first was a surprising and somewhat controversial one. He was far from the best Negro Leagues player at the time—not even close. There were many better players, and quite a few of them could have filled that role capably, but for one reason or another—age, background, education, upbringing—Rickey chose Robinson, and how can you argue with the job Jackie did? He did a fabulous job of paving the way for others to follow.

Robinson had played just part of one season—only two or three months—with the Kansas City Monarchs in the Negro American League. I was still in the army at the time, so I never saw him play with the Monarchs, but I heard a lot about him. The first time I saw him play was when he was with Montreal in 1946 and they came to Jersey City.

With the Monarchs, Robinson played shortstop (the reason I'm picking him as my number one second baseman is because of what he did in the major leagues, what he might have done in the Negro Leagues, and, of course, for his historical significance), batted a torrid .387, and stole 13 bases but hit only five home runs and drove in 23 runs in 47 games.

It just seemed that all the stars were aligned properly for Robinson to break baseball's color barrier. He was young (28 years, two months, and 43 days—just entering his prime years as an athlete—when he debuted with the Dodgers); he came with a built-in reputation as an athlete (a four-sport star at UCLA, where he was accustomed to playing in front of huge, mostly white, crowds); he was educated; he was an army veteran, having been discharged with the rank of second lieutenant; he was intelligent, very eloquent, mentally tough, courageous, and moral; and he had a good marriage.

So how are you going to question Rickey's choice of Robinson? He picked the right person. Jackie was perfect for pioneering. He wasn't the best player, but he was the one best prepared to do the job that he was supposed to do.

*I*n 1964, one year before his death and 17 years after Jackie Robinson joined the Brooklyn Dodgers, Branch Rickey was asked to reflect on breaking baseball's long-standing color line and to discuss the then-current status of African Americans in the United Sates. The following was his response:

A lot of time has passed since Jackie Robinson's first contract was signed. Now I wish to make some observations about Negroes in baseball and out.

I once had a farm club in the little Georgia League; I had five Negroes on the Dublin club. And there was no trouble. Trouble, trouble, trouble, people go looking for trouble, saying there's going to be a civil war. By Judas Priest...it reminds me of when we trained in Panama in '47 and I had the Brooklyn club down there. A lieutenant colonel who had charge of the locks and his sergeant would push buttons and pull levers and ships would come through. I wanted to see the ships come through and made an appointment, and Mother [Mrs. Rickey] and I went there.

The lieutenant colonel said, "Mr. Rickey, would you like to bring that ship through?"

I looked. There were [sic] a great big ship and half a dozen little ones. "That big ship?" I asked.

He said, "Yes."

"Do you mean that enormous battleship? Through here?"

"Yes."

I thought he was kidding. I kept looking and looking. "It can't be done," I said.

"It'll go through," he said.

So I sat down before the buttons and levers, and I did this, and I did that. The first thing I knew, the water began to rise and it rose and rose, and things moved, and within a few minutes the battleship began to move. I give you my word—the opening was so small that it was like passing a camel through the eye of a needle, the most son-of-a-bitching undertaking I'd ever heard of in all my life.

"This can't be," I said to myself. "This is going to be a terrible catastrophe."

But the big ship came on, and went through the opening, and moved steadily, slowly—it looked as if it was rubbing sides both ways. And it went by me with the same slow, deliberate speed that integration is moving in American life today and into the future. And there was that ship, loaded to the gills, in the Atlantic Ocean, where it had just been in the Pacific, on its damnable voyage of destiny to the ports of the world.

Trouble is what they predicted, disasters—"Look what you're getting into!"

And when we got there in baseball it wasn't there!

But you've got to be sure you're right before you move ahead. Then opposition falls, like chips from the axe. And you've won the game, you're on top, just as sure as little green apples grow bigger. That's what this civil rights battle is now. It's a tempest in a teapot, but in a hell of a big teapot.

I would make no change in my policies in respect to breaking the color line if I had to do it all over again. My first problem was to find a player who would represent the finest qualities of the Negro people and, at the same time, be an athlete of the first water. I did, in Jackie Robinson. My second problem was to reconcile him and the hundreds of thousands of others, all white, with whom he would associate or before whom he would play.

My third problem was the Negro people. I anticipated overaddulation of Jackie, mass Negro attendance, gifts, awards—all natural, understandable, the reaction of people who had been down and out for years and years. And, all of a sudden, someone of their own had come into public view, with class, with distinction. "Do you mean to say," they asked me, "that we can't praise him, can't honor him?" Not so! I didn't blame 'em.... I'd have been one of 'em too. I went to three meetings of Brooklyn Negro leaders—they were wonderful, wonderfully understanding and cooperative.

Then there was the hotel situation. Robinson's being unable to stay with the club in certain cities. Wrong! Wrong! How prevent a young man like Robinson from demanding his rights? He was direct, aggressive, the kind that stands up when he is faced with injustice and will hit you right in the snoot. It's understandable—I would be that way, too, and so would any man that's a man!

Now, as I see it today, the main complaint of Negro ball players is that integration in baseball will never be complete until there's integration everywhere—and there certainly is no integration in the Southern places where they train in the spring. Some say that Negroes are happier and more comfortable in spring training being together and not going out with white boys in communities where there is obvious discrimination in spirit. There may be some who would rather be segregated in Florida than go to restaurants and other public places where the evidences of discrimination are so patent. I can understand that. But this Negro moderate, this compromiser, he is hurting his people a very great deal. There should be no compromise on the part of the Negro people in this country. That's my opinion!

There should still be improvement as regards the attitude of Negro ballplayers. Negro ballplayers represent equality of rights before the American people. They should endure discomforts and embarrassment by going into segregated places to prove that it can be done. The average Negro is not yet up to snuff in education with the white people of this country. How could he be? He hasn't had the opportunity. All he needs is to equip himself with complete insistence that he get his rights—and no compromise!

The Negro leadership is conducting itself with perfect propriety in this struggle. Take Whitney Young Jr. of the Urban League—where is there an intellect to surpass his? Or Reverend Martin Luther King? I can name 50 outstanding minds among Negroes today, university masters, Phi Beta Kappas, they're all over the place.

The big challenge to the Negro today is to fight for the right to be equal and then to qualify as an equal. And no less important is the challenge not to compromise for less than equality.

When Jackie signed we were all rooting like crazy for him to succeed, because we knew what it would mean for all of us. At the same time, we weren't jealous of him, but we were envious. There's a difference. Jealousy is when somebody has something that you feel belongs to you; envy is when somebody is in a position you wish you were in. We followed Jackie, and we wished him well, but we wished it had happened 10 years sooner, because they would have gotten the cream of the crop then.

Like Willie Mays four years later, Robinson got off to a very slow start with the Dodgers, which is understandable considering the taunts and slurs he was forced to endure and the tremendous pressure he was under.

But the Dodgers stayed with him, and he wound up batting a respectable .297, hitting 12 home runs, driving in 48 runs, scoring 125 runs, leading the National League with 29 stolen bases, being voted as the first Rookie of the Year (a new award established that year), and helping the Dodgers win their first pennant in six years.

Robinson wasn't a great player when the Dodgers got him, but he just kept improving. So many good players surrounded Jackie; he was fortunate to be in that element.

When the Dodgers moved him from first base to second base and he teamed with Pee Wee Reese, that was a great combination. They worked so well together, and Pee Wee helped Jackie so much, on and off the field. There is a famous incident that happened in Cincinnati during a lull in play; Reese and Robinson were standing near second base talking. As an impulse, Reese threw his arm around Jackie's shoulder. Intentional or not, the gesture spoke volumes. Here was Reese, a southerner from nearby Louisville, Kentucky, telling the world that this black man was his teammate and he supported him completely. It was a bold and courageous act on Reese's part.

Once he got his confidence and started improving, Jackie became so thrilling and exhilarating on the bases: rounding first base on a single, going halfway to second base, and then going back to first; daring outfielders to throw behind him so he could dash to the next base. And he stole home a bunch of times. He became sensational.

When they started barnstorming, people would flock to see Jackie Robinson, and rightly so, because he was the first; he was the leader, so to speak. But we didn't need a leader.

I never had any real relationship with Robinson, but I never had any trouble with him, either. You have to remember that I was playing for the Giants and Robinson was playing for the Dodgers, our archrivals, so we had an adversarial relationship for that reason. Us Giants didn't want to be too friendly with him because Leo Durocher was our manager and he and Jackie had had some problems. So if I saw him on the field, I'd say, "Hello, Jack, how are you?" and just keep on going. After all, I had *Giants* written across the front of my jersey, and he had *Dodgers* written across the front of his.

In that first year, Jackie was under wraps, and you have to admire him for that. Once the wraps came off, he became very aggressive. Some might say abrasive. But after what he went through that first year, if anybody earned the right to be abrasive, he did.

Jackie's aggressiveness and his courage opened many doors that had been previously closed to blacks, and once he opened them, it allowed the rest of us to follow. When Hank Thompson and I joined the Giants in 1948, African Americans were still not accepted in the hotels where the teams stayed, so we'd get to a town and the rest of the team would go to their hotel and we'd take a cab and go to a hotel in the black section of town, or we'd stay with black families.

This went on for several years, and in 1954 Jackie and Don Newcombe went into the Chase Hotel in St. Louis, walked into the restaurant, and sat down. The waiter came over and said, "What do you guys want?"

Jackie said, "We want to get served just like everybody else."

The waiter said, "I'm going to have to call the manager."

The manager came over, and Jackie told him the same thing.

The manager thought for a moment, and then he said, "Well, why not?"

And that opened things up. Soon the Chase Hotel integrated, and the hotels in Chicago and Cincinnati followed suit. That's when everything opened up, because of a simple thing like Robinson and Newcombe having the courage to walk into the restaurant in the Chase Hotel and, without making a scene or a big deal about it, ask to be served.

Not only did Robinson break down the barrier in baseball, his presence in major league baseball had a wide-ranging effect. He made things better for African American football players, basketball players, golfers, and tennis players. He made it possible for young black women who graduated from high school and college to earn jobs as secretaries and in other professions. He made it good for us all around. I give him credit for that.

The last time I saw Jackie was at Game 2 of the 1972 World Series between the Reds and Oakland Athletics in Cincinnati.

When he retired, Robinson continued to rail against baseball for its failure to hire African Americans in front-office management positions and on-field managing and coaching positions. He took several jobs, all of them outside of baseball. He was an executive with the Chock full o'Nuts coffee company and a member of the New York State Athletic Commission, but he boycotted baseball. He never showed up at baseball functions or attended games.

40

Robinson's boycott bothered my boss, Commissioner Bowie Kuhn. It so happened that 1972 was the 25th anniversary of Robinson breaking the color barrier with the Dodgers, and Bowie came up with the idea of commemorating the anniversary by having Jackie attend the World Series. Kuhn reached out to Robinson, but Jackie declined at first. Kuhn persisted. He asked Robinson to at least meet him for lunch so they could discuss the issues Jackie had with baseball.

Jackie agreed to the lunch, and Kuhn apparently convinced him that he was sincere in trying to get more blacks in management positions, because a few days later Robinson agreed to attend the World Series game in Cincinnati.

I was a little shocked when I saw him. His hair was all white, and he was practically blind from the ravages of diabetes, but he still had that fire in him. At the ceremony honoring him, he made a speech and took a not-so-subtle swipe at baseball for not having blacks in the front office or as managers.

Nine days later, we got word that Robinson was dead. He was only 53.

Less than three years later, Frank Robinson was named manager of the Cleveland Indians, the first black manager in major league history. There is no doubt that his hiring came about as an outgrowth of Kuhn and Jackie's luncheon meeting and Jackie's attendance at the World Series.

Although Jackie wasn't in Cleveland's Municipal Stadium on April 8, 1975, for Frank Robinson's first game as manager of the Indians, his wife, Rachel, attended, and Jackie was there in spirit. Once again, he was instrumental in breaking down barriers.

There was a time when people thought that **Sammy T. Hughes** might become the one to break baseball's color line. That's how good a player and fine an individual he was: a guy who played the game hard and with intelligence, what they call a "thinking man's player."

In the 1930s and the first half of the 1940s, Sammy T. was the top second baseman in the Negro Leagues, maybe the best ever (I never saw Bingo DeMoss, but I'm told he was a tremendous second baseman). Hughes made the All-Star team six times, more than any other second baseman. Baseball people who saw him play compare Hughes to Billy Herman and Red Schoendienst, who are both in the Hall of Fame.

Hughes was tall for a second baseman, 6'3", 190 pounds, and wiry, but his height was actually an asset. He could reach balls that other second basemen couldn't. He could field like crazy, with great range and a great arm. Like

Sammy T. Hughes, shown making a play at second base, was one of the slickest-fielding players to ever man second. *Photo courtesy of AP/Wide World Photos.*

Billy Herman, he was the ideal number two hitter in the lineup, a good bunter, an outstanding hit–and–run man, and a good contact hitter who rarely struck out. And he had some pop in his bat. Sammy was a good base runner. He didn't have the flair on the bases that Jackie Robinson had, but in the Negro Leagues, Hughes was a better all-around player than Jackie was. It wasn't until later, after he joined the Dodgers, that Jackie became a great player.

In 1943 there was talk that Hughes, Roy Campanella, and Dave Barnhill were going to get tryouts with the Pittsburgh Pirates, but unfortunately it turned out to be just talk.

Hughes was a candidate for the Hall of Fame recently, but he didn't get enough votes. It's a shame, because I believe he belongs. He was a great player and a great fellow. One thing that seems to have worked against him is that Sammy spent most of his years with the Baltimore Elite Giants and was overshadowed by Campy and Biz Mackey.

The other unfortunate thing about Sammy T. Hughes is that by the time the major league's color barrier finally was broken in 1947, he was 36 years old and past his prime. He had gone into the army during World War II, and when he was discharged in 1946, he was no longer the player he once was and he lost his second-base job to Junior Gilliam.

If there was ever any doubt that Sammy T. could have been a fine major league player, it was erased when he batted .353 in exhibition games against major leaguers.

I once asked the great Negro Leagues shortstop Willie Wells who the best second baseman he played with was, and without hesitation, Willie said **Newt Allen**.

Wells said that Allen could make all the plays and that he was terrific at turning the double play. Willie said that on the double play he would give Allen the ball and Newt didn't even have to look at first base, he could just flip it over his shoulder and make the double play without ever looking at his target.

Allen's best years came before my time, but I'm not going to question Willie Wells. From what I learned from Wells, what Sammy T. Hughes was in the 1930s and 1940s, Newt Allen was in the 1920s—the best second baseman in the Negro Leagues and a fantastic fielder.

In my opinion, Hughes was better than Allen. Sammy T. could do everything that Newt could do on defense, plus Sammy was a better hitter, a home-run hitter. He had more power than Allen.

Newt was a little guy, only 5'7", your typical top-of-the-order hitter. He was a switch-hitter who would slap the ball around, and he was a great bunter. He could run and steal a base, and he was very aggressive on the bases, willing to give up his body to break up a double play. He was scrappy, an Eddie Stanky type of player, but he ran much better than Stanky did.

Newt Allen was another slick-fielding second baseman, a scrappy, top-of-the-order guy similar to the majors' Eddie Stanky. *Photo courtesy of the Rucker Archive.*

44

Allen also was a team leader. He was the captain of the great Kansas City Monarchs team that reached the Negro Leagues World Series in 1924 and 1925. Later Newt became manager of the Monarchs and won five pennants from 1937 to 1942.

Next to Jackie Robinson and Larry Doby, who was a second baseman with the Newark Eagles, Jim "Junior" Gilliam is the best known and most successful of the Negro Leagues second basemen.

Jim Gilliam had a wonderful major league career—all with the Dodgers, in Brooklyn and Los Angeles—and then was a longtime coach for the Dodgers. In 14 seasons he batted .265, had almost 2,000 hits, scored more than 1,000 runs, and stole more than 200 bases. But I can't rate him ahead of Sammy T. Hughes or Newt Allen, which tells you how good Hughes and Allen were and what they might have accomplished if they had come along later and had the opportunity Gilliam had.

Junior was terrific. He was an excellent leadoff hitter in front of those Dodgers teams that had all those sluggers. He was always getting on base, stealing bases, scoring runs. He was a clutch-hitter and a switch-hitter with some power. When Don Larsen pitched his perfect game in the 1956 World Series, Gilliam hit a foul home run that just missed the left-field foul pole to lead off the seventh inning. A few inches to the right and the perfect game would have been ruined.

Gilliam was not yet 17 when he joined the Baltimore Elite Giants in 1945 and teamed with shortstop Pee Wee Butts to form one of the great double-play combinations in Negro Leagues history. (What a coincidence that a few years later with the Dodgers, Junior teamed with another Pee Wee—Reese—to form another great double-play combination.) Junior made the Negro National League East All-Star team three straight years, from 1948 to 1950, and then he was signed by the Dodgers and sent to Montreal.

In Montreal he led the International League in runs in 1951 and again in 1952, when he also led the league's second basemen in fielding percentage. His accomplishments convinced the Dodgers to bring Gilliam to Brooklyn and to move Jackie Robinson, who was getting older and slowing down because of knee problems, to third base.

Gilliam broke into the big leagues with a bang. He batted .278, set a National League rookie record with 100 walks, led the league in triples with 17, was fourth in runs scored with 125 (a career high), played excellent second base, and was named NL Rookie of the Year. He also batted .296 in the World Series and hit two home runs, one left-handed and one right-handed.

Junior scored at least 100 runs in each of his first four major league seasons, and three times—in 1956, 1957, and 1959—he finished second to Willie Mays in steals.

When the Dodgers moved to Los Angeles in 1958, Gilliam became an immediate hit with the fans on the West Coast, leading the Dodgers in hits, doubles, steals, walks, and fielding average in their first year in L.A. When he started to slow down because of age, Gilliam moved to other positions and became the Dodgers' all-around handy man, playing several positions.

In his career, Gilliam played more than 1,000 games at second base, more than 700 at third base, and more than 200 in the outfield, and he even got in two games as a first baseman. When the Dodgers won the pennant in 1965, Junior, at the age of 36, batted .280 in 111 games and was part of the only all-switch-hitting infield in major league history, made up of Wes

After three straight All-Star seasons in the Negro Leagues, Jim Gilliam succeeded Jackie Robinson at second base for the Dodgers and was named the National League Rookie of the Year in 1953.

Parker at first base, Jim Lefebvre at second, Maury Wills at shortstop, and Gilliam at third.

No surprise to me, Gilliam was one of the most popular Dodgers in Los Angeles. He was a good fellow, just a great guy to have on a team, and a fun-loving guy. He was a great cardplayer and a great pool shooter. He and Willie Mays both were great at pool. Leo Durocher taught Willie how to play pool, and Mays got to the point where he could beat Gilliam.

Walter Alston loved Gilliam. He made Junior his third-base coach after Gilliam retired in 1966. Gilliam held that job for the next 11 years, and then, just a couple of days before the start of the 1978 World Series between the Dodgers and the Yankees, Junior suffered a brain hemorrhage and died. He was only 50 years old.

The Dodgers retired Gilliam's No. 19, and they say that the only time anybody ever saw Walter Alston cry was at Junior's funeral.

Lorenzo Davis was born in Alabama, in a suburb of Birmingham, a little town called Piper. And that explains how he got the nickname that remained with him for the rest of his 80 years.

In high school, **Piper Davis** was such a good all-around athlete that he earned a basketball scholarship to Alabama State University. But after one year, Piper had to leave school and get a job to help out with his family's finances. He took a job with a Birmingham steel mill and played for the mill's baseball team, an all-black team.

In 1942 Davis joined the Birmingham Black Barons. Their manager, Winfield Welch, also happened to be the coach of the famous Harlem Globetrotters basketball team. Welch had heard about Davis's basketball skills and invited him to join the 'Trotters, which Piper did.

Meanwhile, Davis's baseball career was flourishing. He teamed with Ed Steele and Artie Wilson to give the Black Barons the most powerful team in the Negro American League during the 1940s. Four times during the 1940s, he was named to the West squad in the annual East-West Negro Leagues All-Star Game. But Piper never abandoned his love for basketball or his basketball career. For years he played baseball during the summer and then joined the Globetrotters after the baseball season.

In 1948, when the Black Barons switched to the Negro National League (NNL), they made Davis their player/manager. He continued to play at an All-Star level and managed the Black Barons to the NNL pennant, but despite his success on the field and in the dugout, he is best known for signing a 16-year-old Birmingham kid named Willie Mays.

In 1950 Davis became the first African American to sign a contract with the Boston Red Sox, the last major league team to integrate. The Red Sox paid the Black Barons $15,000, the most ever paid to sign a black player at the time, and sent Piper to Scranton (Pennsylvania) in the Class A Eastern League. He got as far as Triple A ball and played five years with the Oakland Oaks of the Pacific Coast League but never reached the major leagues. At the age of 41, he was player/manager for the Fort Worth Cats of the Double A Texas League. It was Piper's last year in organized baseball.

But he would continue to be a presence in Major League Baseball for the next quarter century, serving as a scout for the Tigers, Cardinals, and Expos before retiring in 1986. Seven years later, Davis was inducted into the Alabama Sports Hall of Fame.

47

Piper Davis was a terrific second baseman and eventually a player/ manager for the Birmingham Black Barons, for whom he signed a 16-year-old Birmingham kid named Willie Mays.

48

I want to make special mention here of George Scales, who played with several teams, including the St. Louis Stars, Lincoln Giants, Homestead Grays, New York Black Yankees, and Baltimore Elite Giants (he also managed the latter two). Scales was a very intelligent player who made up for his lack of speed with his savvy. George was probably better known for his bat than for his glove, and I remember him as an excellent curveball hitter. When I saw him, he was on the way down, but he still could hit the curveball.

Career Summaries

Second Baseman	Years	Teams
Jackie Robinson *Scored 36 runs in 47 games for Monarchs in 1945*	1945	Kansas City Monarchs
Sammy T. Hughes *Batted over .300 six times*	1930–46	Louisville White Sox, Nashville/Columbus/Washington/Baltimore Elite Giants, Washington Pilots
Newt Allen *Had 14 four-hit games and twice had five hits in a game*	1922–47	Kansas City Monarchs, St. Louis Stars, Homestead Grays, Indianapolis Clowns
Jim Gilliam *Led league with 13 triples and 94 runs in 1949*	1945–51	Baltimore Elite Giants
Piper Davis *Hit .462 in four East-West All-Star Games*	1942–50	Birmingham Black Barons

FOUR

Shortstop

Think of Ozzie Smith without the flips. That was **Willie Wells**. In the field he could do everything Ozzie Smith did—you can't get any higher praise than that—and he was a much better hitter than Ozzie was. Willie was a great curveball hitter, a lifetime .300 hitter who won the Negro National League batting title in 1930 with a .403 average. And he had pretty good power for a little guy, about 5'8" tall and 170 pounds.

When I joined the Newark Eagles, Wells was their shortstop. He was in his midthirties, and he was still the best shortstop in the league. He was spectacular. He was the best I've ever seen at going back and catching Texas Leaguers.

Willie had unbelievable range and amazingly sure hands. He didn't have a great arm, but he had a quick release and an accurate arm. Phil Rizzuto's throws to first base always seemed to beat the runner by a half step—that's how Willie Wells's throws were. He'd get rid of the ball quickly, and his throw was always right on the money, a half step ahead of the runner.

1. WILLIE WELLS

2. POP LLOYD

3. ERNIE BANKS

4. DICK LUNDY

5. JOHN BECKWITH

The Eagles signed me as a shortstop, but with Wells there, I wasn't going to get to play very much. And yet I owe him a debt of gratitude because it was Willie who said I belonged in the outfield, so that's where I went, and that's where I played throughout my major league career. Who knows if I ever would have made it as a shortstop?

Willie Wells would get rid of the ball quickly, and his throw was always right on the money, a half step ahead of the runner.

With the Eagles, Wells became the centerpiece in what was called the Million Dollar Infield (in reality, it was more like the $1,000-per-month infield): Mule Suttles at first base, Dick Seay at second, Wells at short, and Ray Dandridge at third.

Willie made the Negro Leagues All-Star team eight times, which is all the more remarkable when you realize that in his first nine seasons—his best years—there was no Negro Leagues All-Star team.

Wells might have been the first baseball player ever to wear a batting helmet. He had been hit in the head by a pitch and suffered a concussion, but he refused to be taken out of the lineup. Instead, he continued to play by getting a construction worker's hard hat and wearing it when he came to bat.

In 1940 Willie went to Mexico to play for Veracruz and dazzled the Mexicans just as he dazzled fans and opponents in the Negro Leagues. He batted .345 in 1940 and .347 in 1947, but it was his glove that drew raves. The Mexicans called him *"el Diablo,"* the Devil. They'd say, "Don't hit the ball to the Devil; hit it someplace else. The Devil's playing shortstop. Hit it the other way, because he'll go get the ball and throw you out."

After two years in Mexico, Wells came back to Newark and was player/manager for the Eagles.

The sad part of Willie Wells's story is that he never had the opportunity to show his enormous talent on the big stage, the major leagues. In exhibition games against major leaguers, Wells batted .410 and earned the respect and admiration of Charlie Gehringer, the Detroit Tigers' great Hall of Fame second baseman, who years later said, "Wells played the way all great players play, with everything he had. He was the kind of player you always wanted on your team."

I regret that Willie never got the chance to show what he could do, that the world never got to see the ballplayer I saw. He would have been a major star.

Willie Wells was as gifted a defensive shortstop as has ever played the game, and he was a terrific hitter as well.

But no major league owner wanted him or had the courage to sign him when he was at the top of his game. By the time Jackie Robinson broke in with the Dodgers in 1947, Willie was 42 years old. I can only imagine how Wells felt knowing there were major league shortstops who, as the saying goes, couldn't carry his glove. At least Wells had the satisfaction that when the Dodgers signed Robinson and were going to convert him from shortstop to second base, they asked Willie to tutor Jackie on making the pivot at second base on double plays.

Willie took great pride in Robinson's success and in the fact that three of the players he managed with the Newark Eagles—Larry Doby, Don Newcombe, and a fellow named Monte Irvin—had productive major league careers.

Wells continued to play until 1949 and finally hung up his spikes at the age of 44. He died in 1989 and never even had the joy of seeing his plaque hang in Cooperstown. He was voted into the Hall of Fame posthumously in 1997.

Playing his first season of semipro baseball as a teenager, Grant Johnson reportedly blasted 60 balls out of the park, thereby earning him the nickname "Home Run" Johnson, which he carried throughout his playing career. Johnson's career lasted until 1932, when he played for the Buffalo Giants at the age of 58.

An outstanding shortstop and hitter, Johnson also was known as a student of the game who said that the two primary requisites for batting were confidence and fearlessness. He also preached that when a game was on the line, a pitcher would rather face "the mighty swinger than the cool steady batter who tries to meet the ball and place it to the best advantage."

Despite his nickname, Johnson practiced what he preached. In 1910 he batted .397 for the Leland Giants, a team that won an astonishing 123 out of 129 games. From 1911 to 1913, Johnson batted .374, .413, and .371 for the Lincoln Giants.

However, his greatest accomplishment came while he was playing for the Havana Reds in 1910. In a 12-game series against a touring group of major leaguers, Johnson batted .412 and outhit both 12-time American League batting champion Ty Cobb and his Detroit Tigers teammate Hall of Famer "Wahoo" Sam Crawford.

They called him "the black Honus Wagner" for a couple of reasons: He was a shortstop. He was the best player in his league in his time.

His time was long ago—long, long ago. John Henry Lloyd was born into poverty in Palatka, Florida, in 1884. His father died when John Henry was an infant. His mother remarried and sent John Henry to live with his grandmother.

Lloyd left school before completing the elementary grades in order to help with the finances by taking on odd jobs. He worked as a delivery boy for a local general store and discovered baseball. In 1905 he caught on as a catcher with the Macon (Georgia) Acmes, a team so poor that it didn't have a catcher's mask or chest protector, so Lloyd went behind the plate protected by only a glove.

One day, he took a foul tip on his left eye, which afterward began to close. John Henry spit on his finger, rubbed it on the lid, and continued catching. Four innings later, a foul tip caught him on his right eye, and John Henry announced to his teammates, "Gentleman, I guess I'll have to quit; I can't see the ball."

That was the end of John Henry Lloyd's career as a catcher.

I saw **Pop Lloyd** play one time in East Orange, New Jersey, in 1930, but I was only 11 years old and he was well past his prime—he must have been close to 50 years old at the time—and playing first base by then, so I don't remember anything about him. But anybody who has done any research into Negro Leagues baseball, or who was around when he played, knows about John Henry Lloyd, who, in his latter years, was affectionately called "Pop."

I never saw him play in his prime, but many who did called John Henry "Pop" Lloyd the greatest player in any league, anywhere.

Some people say he was the greatest African American player ever. That may be so—I don't know—but what seems to be clear is that he was the best black player of his time, just as Wagner was the best white player of his.

Connie Mack once said, "Put Lloyd and Wagner in the same bag, and whichever one you pulled out, you couldn't go wrong." Wagner, himself, said, "I am honored to have John Lloyd called the black Wagner. It is a privilege to have been compared with him."

"Put Lloyd and [Honus] Wagner in the same bag, and whichever one you pulled out, you couldn't go wrong."
—Connie Mack.

Lloyd was a brilliant fielder and a devastating left-handed hitter with power. He played in the Negro Leagues for 26 years, until the age of 47, and after he "retired," he was active organizing and promoting youth baseball in Atlantic City, New Jersey, and continued to play on Atlantic City's semipro fields until the age of 58.

Lloyd played 12 seasons in Cuba, where he was known as *"el Cuchara"*—the Shovel—because of his habit of scooping up handfuls of infield dirt when digging out ground balls.

In 1910 the Detroit Tigers traveled to Cuba for a series of 12 games against a team of Cuban All-Stars. Ty Cobb played in five of the games and batted .369. Lloyd played in all 12 games, batted .500, and also tagged out Cobb trying to steal second base three times. In 29 games against major leaguers for which records are available, Pop batted .321.

During a radio interview with the great broadcaster Graham McNamee, Babe Ruth was asked who he believed was the greatest player of all time.

"You mean major leagues?" Babe asked.

"No," said McNamee, "the greatest player anywhere."

"In that case," Ruth replied, "I'd pick John Henry Lloyd."

From what people have told me, Lloyd was a great person, very intelligent and soft-spoken, an elegant and dignified gentleman who never drank, never smoked, and never cussed. He was a complete professional on and off the field.

There's a foundation named for John Henry Lloyd in Atlantic City. Every year they have a dinner to remember this great man.

Until his death, Pop Lloyd was revered as the elder statesman of Negro Leagues baseball. He died in 1965, 12 years before he was inducted into the Hall of Fame.

In 1950 the Kansas City Monarchs signed a tall, skinny 19-year-old infielder from Dallas named **Ernie Banks** and made him their shortstop. After one season with the Monarchs, Banks was drafted into the army. When he was discharged two years later, he returned to the Monarchs, after which the Chicago Cubs signed him and brought him directly to Chicago—without a stop in the minor leagues—for 10 games at the end of the 1953 season. A year later he was the Cubs' regular shortstop, teaming with another Negro Leagues alumnus, Gene Baker, to give the Cubs the first all-black double-play combination in major league history.

In 1955 Banks hit 44 home runs, a major league record for a shortstop and third in the National League, and drove in 117 runs, fourth in the league: a Hall of Fame career was under way.

Upon signing with the Cubs after his stint with the Kansas City Monarchs, Ernie Banks teamed with Gene Baker in 1954 to form the first all-black double-play combination in the major leagues.

Over the next seven seasons, Banks would hit 270 home runs and twice lead the league. He was such a dominant player that he won back-to-back National League Most Valuable Player awards in 1958 and 1959 on teams that finished in fifth place both times.

Although Ernie wasn't the best fielding shortstop of his time in the major leagues, he wasn't the worst, either. I would say he was more than adequate as a shortstop, with good range and a good arm. And could he hit! He had those amazingly quick hands and quick wrists. They used to say that he had such quick wrists he could hit a ball practically out of the catcher's mitt and drive it over the fence.

By 1962, when Ernie had passed age 30 and began to slow down in the field and couldn't cover the ground he once did, the Cubs switched him to first base. He played there for 10 years and continued to hit home runs, finishing with 512, 10th on the all-time list at the time.

I joined the Cubs in my final year in the big leagues, 1956, and I played with Ernie when he was just going into his prime. He was the main man then—and a good teammate: always on time, always upbeat, always wanting to do the right thing. A great team guy. "Let's play two," he'd say. "And if that's not enough, let's play three."

When I joined the Cubs, I was using a Louisville Slugger S2 model bat that had been designed for Vern Stephens back in 1943. I thought this bat was one Ernie would like, so I showed it to him and suggested that he try it. He did, and he liked it. That was the model he used for the rest of his career, so I'm proud to say that Banks hit most of his 512 home runs using the bat model I suggested to him.

Ernie being Ernie, he has never forgotten that I turned him on to that model. It's some 50 years later, and still every time I see him, he says, "Monte, thank you for introducing me to the S2. I don't think I would have hit as many home runs as I did without that bat."

Ernie was, and always will be, Mr. Cub, and deservedly so. He's the most popular player in Cubs history, just a delightful guy to be around.

I have the greatest respect for Ernie as a man and as a player, and I'm happy for his success. The only thing that bothers me is that as good as Banks was, there were better shortstops in the Negro Leagues, at least defensively, and they never got their chance.

Dick Lundy's career was sandwiched between Pop Lloyd's and Willie Wells's, and most consider them the three best shortstops in Negro Leagues history. *Photo courtesy of the Rucker Archive.*

Among the great Negro Leagues shortstops that never got a chance was **Dick Lundy**. You don't hear much about him. He isn't even in the Hall of Fame, but he should be.

Lundy's career was sandwiched between Pop Lloyd's and Willie Wells's, and those three are regarded as the greatest shortstops in Negro Leagues history.

Dick was my first manager when I joined the Newark Eagles in 1938—a great guy. He was 40 years old then and on the downgrade, but he was still a pretty good player, and people told me how good he had been.

They called him "King Richard" he was so good: a great, great shortstop, a good switch-hitter, and a terrific base runner. He was a natural leader who was respected by teammates and opponents alike for his quiet leadership, so much so that at the age of 27, he was named player/manager of the Bacharach Giants.

The careers of Dick Lundy and **John Beckwith** overlapped. Although Beckwith wasn't in the same class as Lundy, Willie Wells, or Pop Lloyd as a fielder, they tell me he was second to none as a power hitter.

Beckwith was big and strong, a right-handed slugger who weighed 230 pounds, which is very unusual for a shortstop, and he hit some of the longest and most talked about home runs in Negro Leagues baseball. "Double Duty" Radcliffe once said that nobody hit the ball farther than Beckwith, not even Josh Gibson, whose home runs were legendary.

When he was 19, Beckwith became the first player, black or white, to hit a ball over the laundry behind the left-field fence in Crosley Field (Cincinnati). And they say that in Washington's Griffith Stadium, Beckwith hit a ball beyond the left-field bleachers that hit a billboard 460 feet from home plate and 40 feet high.

Beckwith's fatal flaws were a tendency to be a little lazy in the field and a fiery temper and mean disposition. I've heard that in one game, Beckwith made an error that cost pitcher Bill Holland a ballgame and so enraged Holland that he threw his glove on the ground in disgust. Angry that he was being shown up by a teammate, Beckwith walked over to Holland and decked him with his right hand.

Beckwith never won a batting championship, but three times he finished as runner-up to the champion. He did win two home-run titles, but on two other occasions he again was forced to play the role of bridesmaid when he missed winning the home-run crown by a single homer each time, and both times to the great Oscar Charleston.

It's tough to choose between Pop Lloyd, Willie Wells, Dick Lundy, and John Beckwith. They just had all this natural ability, and they never dwelled on the fact that they never had a chance or that they never made enough money. They just went out and played. Maybe things would get better later, they said. In the meantime, let's play ball.

Things did get better later, but for those four great players, it was too late.

Other Negro Leagues shortstops worthy of mention are Dobie Moore, who was before my time, but they tell me he was the equal of Willie Wells as a fielder; "Home Run" Johnson; and Sam Bankhead, the brother of Dan, who was the first black pitcher in the major leagues with the Brooklyn Dodgers. Sam was a great outfielder who moved to shortstop and was more than adequate.

There were also Bill Yancey, a light hitter but a good fielder and a great instructor; Charlie Neal; a couple of guys nicknamed Pee Wee—Frank Austin and Thomas Butts, the latter a very fine fielder and good hitter and a teammate of Roy Campanella's with the Baltimore Elite Giants; and my old New York Giants teammate Artie Wilson, a great fellow who was a star in the Negro Leagues as a fielder and a hitter. Artie never was the player in the major leagues that he had been in the Negro Leagues. Leo Durocher loved him, but Artie just couldn't pull the ball. A left-handed hitter, he would hit everything to left field. I used to talk to him about it, try to get him to pull the ball, but he just couldn't do it.

Career Summaries

Shortstop	Years	Teams
Willie Wells *Blasted 27 home runs in 1929, tying Mule Suttles's season record*	1924–48	St. Louis Stars, Kansas City Monarchs, Detroit Wolves, Homestead Grays, Chicago American Giants, Newark Eagles, New York Black Yankees, Baltimore Elite Giants, Memphis Red Sox
Pop Lloyd *Collected 11 consecutive hits during 1924 season*	1905–32	Cuban X Giants, Philadelphia Giants, Chicago Leland Giants, New York Lincoln Stars, Chicago American Giants, Brooklyn Royal Giants, New York/Atlantic City Bacharach Giants, Hilldale Daisies, Columbus Buckeyes, Harlem Stars
Ernie Banks *Drove in 47 runs in 46 games for Monarchs in 1953 before joining Cubs*	1950, 1953	Kansas City Monarchs
Dick Lundy *Had six RBIs and six runs scored in 1926 Negro Leagues World Series*	1916–37	Atlantic City Bacharach Giants, Hilldale Daisies, Baltimore Black Sox, Philadelphia Stars, Newark Dodgers, New York Cubans, Newark Eagles

continued	Years	Teams	
John Beckwith *Hit two or more homers in a game six times and four or more RBIs in a game 15 times*	1916–35	Chicago American Giants, Baltimore Black Sox, Harrisburg Giants, Homestead Grays, Lincoln Giants, Newark Browns, New York Black Yankees	

FIVE

Third Baseman

I feel sorry for any true baseball fan who never got to see **Ray Dandridge** play. That fan has no idea what he or she missed. Here was this little (5'7", 175 pounds), squat, bowlegged guy, and he could play third base like Pie Traynor, Brooks Robinson, Mike Schmidt, Graig Nettles, and anybody else you want to name. It was incredible how this man could play third base. And he was a good hitter, too, a good number two hitter. He was just a great, great player.

Ask Tommy Lasorda about Dandridge. Tommy played with him in Cuba, and Lasorda used to get on me for not saying enough about Dandridge. Lasorda said, "When I played with Dandridge, he was always the best player on the team, and he was in his late thirties when I saw him."

1. RAY DANDRIDGE
2. JUDY JOHNSON
3. OLIVER MARCELLE
4. JUD WILSON
5. HENRY THOMPSON

In Cuba they used to say about Dandridge and his bowlegs that "a train might go through his legs, but not a baseball."

Ray came out of Richmond, Virginia, and signed with the Detroit Stars. Later he joined the Newark Eagles, and that's where I got to know him and

Ray Dandridge was as fine a fielding third baseman as I've ever seen. While playing down in Mexico, he actually turned down an offer to go north and play for the Cleveland Indians, but he later said his one regret was never having played a game in the major leagues.

appreciate his talent. He was my teammate, my roommate, my friend, and, in some ways, my mentor. People would pay their way into the ballpark just to see him field.

Third base was Dandridge's primary position, but he was just as good at shortstop and second base. When the Eagles signed Bus Clarkson, a third baseman and a pretty good hitter, they moved Dandridge to second base, and he was almost as good at second as he was at third.

One time when Dandridge was playing second, a ball was hit up the middle, over the bag. Dandridge flashed to his right and backhanded the ball, a spectacular play, but he was on a dead run and out of position to throw to first. So what did he do? He simply flipped the ball to shortstop Willie Wells with his glove hand, and Wells turned it over to first base just in time to nip the runner. I could hardly believe my eyes. It's the first time I had ever seen that play, and if I hadn't seen it with my own eyes, I would never have believed it.

After Jackie Robinson signed with the Dodgers, Bill Veeck contacted Dandridge and tried to sign him for the Cleveland Indians. Ray was playing in Mexico at the time, making pretty good money and enjoying life. He told Veeck that he wouldn't leave Mexico unless the Indians gave him a bonus. Veeck wouldn't do that, so Ray stayed in Mexico and let his chance to play in the major leagues pass him by.

In 1949 Dandridge, who had played 16 seasons in the Negro Leagues and was 36 years old, and pitcher Dave Barnhill of the New York Cubans were signed by the New York Giants and sent to the Minneapolis Millers in the Triple A American Association. They were the first African Americans ever to play for the Millers.

In his first year in organized baseball, Dandridge batted .362. He followed it up by hitting .311 in 1950 and being named American Association Most Valuable Player. The Giants had started the season with Bill Rigney, who would bat .181, and "Lucky" Jack Lohrke, who would hit .186, splitting time at third base. Dandridge certainly would have hit higher than .181 and .186 and would have produced more runs than Rigney or Lohrke did. Players kept telling manager Leo Durocher, "Bring Dandridge up from Minneapolis. He can help us, maybe win a pennant for us."

Leo was willing, but owner Horace Stoneham kept coming up with reasons not to bring Dandridge to New York. First he said Ray was too old. Well, what difference does it make how old a guy is if he can play?

Another excuse he gave was that Dandridge was the most popular player the Millers had, and if they lost him, it would hurt their attendance.

That didn't make sense, either. Isn't the main function of a farm team to produce players for the parent club?

I'm not criticizing Horace Stoneham. He was a terrific man and a fair-minded owner. What I believe is that Horace was under pressure to maintain a quota system. The Giants already had two African Americans—me and Henry Thompson—and a third, Willie Mays, on the fast track to New York.

As it turned out, the Giants put Thompson at third base in 1950, and Hank did a terrific job. He batted .289, hit 20 home runs, and drove in 91 runs. But Thompson was nowhere near the defensive third baseman Dandridge was. We would have been a much better team with Dandridge, even if he was used only as a defensive replacement in late innings. He would have dazzled people with his defense, and he might have saved a few games for us. We finished in third place, five games behind the Phillies. Dandridge's glove might have won us five more games.

Many years later, Dandridge said his one regret in life was that he never played even one game in the major leagues.

Ray went back to Minneapolis in 1951. He was 38 years old, and in his next-to-last season he batted .324 for the Millers. He also took a young player named Willie Mays under his wing and helped him in many ways, on and off the field.

At least the Giants showed their appreciation for Dandridge by giving him a job as a scout, and Ray also had the satisfaction of being elected to the Hall of Fame in 1987, when he was still living. Mays was at Dandridge's induction ceremony in Cooperstown and made a point of telling people, "Ray Dandridge helped me tremendously when I came through Minneapolis. Sometimes you can't overlook those things. Ray was a part of me when I was coming along."

Everything I said about Ray Dandridge—that he was as good of a defensive third baseman as Brooks Robinson, Mike Schmidt, and Graig Nettles—Ted Page, who was an outfielder with the Pittsburgh Crawfords, said about **Judy Johnson**, who preceded Dandridge as the Negro Leagues' top third baseman.

"Judy Johnson was the smartest third baseman I ever came across. A scientific ballplayer, he did everything with grace and poise." —Ted Page

"Judy Johnson was the smartest third baseman I ever came across," Page said. "A scientific ballplayer, he did everything with grace and poise. You talk about playing third base. Heck, he was better than anybody I saw. And I saw Brooks Robinson, Mike Schmidt, and even Pie Traynor. He had a powerful, accurate arm. He could do anything: come in for a ball, cut it off at the line, or range way over toward the shortstop hole. He was really something."

Older players I talked to who saw Johnson play talked about his ability to perform in the clutch, at bat and in the field, and his baseball intelligence. He started out in 1918 with the Bacharach Giants, playing for $5 per game. He batted only .227 in his first year, but Pop Lloyd took a liking to Judy and worked with him, helping Johnson to polish his skills at bat and in the field.

"Pop taught me more baseball than anybody else," Johnson said.

Judy, whose real name was William, moved on to the Hilldale Club and before long was a consistent .300 hitter. In 1923 he batted .391 and led Hilldale to its first Eastern Colored League pennant. The following year, Johnson batted .324 for Hilldale, which met the Kansas City Monarchs in the first Negro Leagues World Series. Judy led all batters with a .364 average, eight

Judy Johnson was the Negro Leagues' best defensive third baseman in the era prior to Ray Dandridge's career, and he also hit .390 to earn MVP honors in 1929.

RBIs, and 16 hits, but the Monarchs prevailed in a 10-game series (there was one tie).

After he was hit in the head by a pitch, Johnson's average slipped below .300 in 1927 and 1928, but he rebounded to hit .390 in 1929, and *The Pittsburgh Courier* named him his league's Most Valuable Player.

Late in his career, Judy bounced around from Hilldale to the Homestead Grays and the Darby Daisies before finishing up his career with the Pittsburgh Crawfords. In 1935 he was named captain of the Crawfords, a team that also had Negro Leagues all-timers Satchel Paige, Cool Papa Bell, and Josh Gibson on its roster.

Johnson died in 1989 at the age of 89. Fourteen years earlier, like Ray Dandridge, he had the satisfaction of seeing his plaque adorn the walls of the Hall of Fame in Cooperstown.

Before Ray Dandridge and Judy Johnson, the top third baseman in the Negro Leagues was **Oliver Marcelle**. I never did see him play, but I heard a lot about him. They called him "the Ghost," and they say he could really play third base. Back in the 1950s, *The Pittsburgh Courier* picked Marcelle as the Negro Leagues' greatest third baseman, ahead of Dandridge and Johnson.

Even Johnson had to agree that Marcelle was his superior as a third baseman—defensively, not offensively. In fact, when Marcelle and Johnson played on the same team in winter ball, Judy moved to second base to allow Marcelle to play third.

Offensively, Marcelle was more of a slashing type hitter, but a good one, especially in the clutch. One year in Cuba, he won a batting title with a .393 average. He also batted .333 in exhibition games against major leaguers.

The Ghost had one big problem. He had a violent temper that often got him into trouble with umpires and scrapes with opponents. One time he got into a dispute with Oscar Charleston and wound up hitting Charleston over the head with a bat.

Although he played for 13 years, Marcelle's career was shortened because of his temper. Ghost was a big, tall, good-looking guy, very vain and very proud. In Cuba he got into a fight with Frank Warfield. They scuffled, and in the mêlée, shades of Mike Tyson and Evander Holyfield, Warfield bit off a piece of Marcelle's nose.

Oliver Marcelle was yet another tremendous third baseman—in fact, some experts rate him higher than both Ray Dandridge and Judy Johnson—but his temper got him into trouble and ultimately shortened his career.

After that, the Ghost was never the same player. He tried wearing a black patch across his nose, but he was so humiliated that he couldn't play anymore, and he just quit.

That reminds me of another player, named Dobie Moore, a shortstop for the Kansas City Monarchs. They say he could really pick it, and what happened to him was that he was shot by his girlfriend. He recovered from the shooting, but he was never the same ballplayer again.

So what I'm saying is that sometimes bad things happen that change a guy's life, and that's what happened to Oliver Marcelle.

I saw **Jud Wilson** at the end of his career—and could he hit. As a third base-man, he was just mediocre, but what a hitter! He was a picturesque left-handed hitter who could hit left-handers. When he came to bat, it was like poetry at the plate. He could hit anybody. All he wanted you to do was just throw it up there.

"They all looked the same to me," he once said.

They called him "Boojum," because players said that's the sound his line drives made when they slammed off outfield walls.

Wilson was another guy, like Oliver Marcelle, who had a temper. He was ready to fight you anywhere, any time. There's a story that Jud once broke

Jud Wilson, who had a .345 career average over 22 seasons in the Negro Leagues, is considered one of the best hitters of all time.

up a knife fight in the showers and another that he got into a scrap with his best friend, Jake Stephens, and Jud grabbed Stephens by the ankles and dangled him out of a hotel window several stories above the ground.

When Jud Wilson came to bat, it was like poetry at the plate. He could hit anybody.

Playing in Cuba, Wilson twice had averages over .400 and had a lifetime average of .372 for six seasons. In the Negro Leagues, his career average was .345 for 22 seasons. Josh Gibson said Wilson was the best hitter in the game, and Satchel Paige called Jud one of the two top hitters he faced in the Negro Leagues. Why not? Jud had a .375 lifetime average against Satch.

Everybody knows that Jackie Robinson was the first African American to play in the major leagues, and most people know that Larry Doby was the second. But not too many remember that my old New York Giants teammate Hank Thompson was the third black player in the major leagues.

Henry Thompson was with the Kansas City Monarchs when he and another Monarch, Willard Brown, were sold to the St. Louis Browns in July 1947, just a few months after Robinson broke the Major League Baseball color line. Doby made his debut with the Cleveland Indians on July 5. Twelve days later, Thompson played his first game for the Browns (Willard Brown would debut two days later).

Hank had started with the Monarchs in 1943 at the age of 17. When the season ended, he was drafted into the army and served as a machine gunner during the Battle of the Bulge. When the war was over, he returned to the Monarchs until he got the call from St. Louis.

Unfortunately, Hank was not ready for the major leagues. He appeared in only 27 games, batted .256 without a home run, had five RBIs, and was released after just 36 days. (Brown played in only 21 games, batted .179 with one home run and six RBIs, and was also released.)

The Browns thought Thompson and Brown would have an impact as Jackie had with the Dodgers and Doby with the Indians, but they were with a bad team and they just never got started. What they should have done was let them play in the minor leagues for a month or two to get their feet on the ground.

Thompson went back to the Monarchs, and he got a second chance (Brown never did) when the New York Giants signed him and sent him to Jersey City in the International League, and he kept improving. Henry and

73

I were teammates in Jersey City, and we were called up to the big leagues together, on July 5, 1949, which I'm sure was not just by happenstance. It had to be planned that we would come up together so we would be each other's roommate, someone to talk to and hang out with. It meant we wouldn't be as lonely as it would have been if one of us had come up alone as Jackie Robinson had.

Hank and I were the first players of color the Giants ever had, and when we arrived Leo Durocher called a clubhouse meeting.

"Hey, men, listen up here," Durocher said. "We've got two new members, Hank and Monte, and I think they can help us. Let me say this: the only thing I'm going to say about color is if you can play baseball and help us win

Henry Thompson was the third black player in the big leagues, but it wasn't until his second chance when he came up with me to the New York Giants that he really played up to his potential.

and make some money, I don't give a damn if you're green, you can play on this team."

Leo was sincere about that, and he showed it in many ways. We had a lot of southerners on the team—Alvin Dark, Eddie Stanky, Whitey Lockman, and Clint Hartung—but we never had any problems with race, and I attribute a lot of that to Durocher and to teammates like Lockman, Bobby Thomson, and Wes Westrum. Those guys were wonderful, and we all got along.

When Willie Mays came along two years later, it made things easier for Hank and me. Willie was such a great youngster; he won over our teammates with his personality and his ability. We used to have a lot of fun in the clubhouse before games. Willie joining the club made things that much more pleasant for us.

Durocher was great at molding his team and getting it to believe in itself. When we were chasing the Dodgers in 1951, I never heard Leo say, "Let's catch them." He always said, "Let's see how close we can come."

Thompson spent eight seasons with the Giants and had some very good years. He played all over the lot—a little second base, a little shortstop, a little third base, and a little outfield—and he was a member of two pennant-winning teams (1951 and 1954) and one World Series champion (1954).

Hank was a left-handed hitter with amazing power for a little guy, only 5'9", 170 pounds. The little fella could play, and he could hit. He's one of the few players to have hit a ball into the center-field seats in Cuba. He got $2,000 for it. With the Giants, he had a career average of .267 with 129 home runs and 477 RBIs in 906 games.

As good as his career was, there's no telling how much better he would have been if he had lived a different lifestyle. Hank liked the nightlife, and he made sure to live it to the maximum. If he got a World Series check, you could be sure that it would be all gone in a few weeks.

Even though he washed out in St. Louis and people don't remember that he was the third African American to play in a major league game, Thompson still made some baseball history.

He was the first black to play in both the American and National Leagues.

When the Browns, with Thompson, played against the Indians, with Doby, in August 1947, it was the first time black players on opposing teams played on the same field in the major leagues.

When Hank batted against the Dodgers' Don Newcombe, it was the first time in major league history a black pitcher faced a black batter.

And when Don Mueller was injured in the third game of the 1951 playoff, Thompson started the 1951 World Series in his place. With Hank in right field, Willie Mays in center, and me in left, that was the first all–African American outfield in major league history, although I never even thought about that at the time.

After Mueller got hurt, we all figured Thompson was the logical choice to replace him in the outfield. It was the right thing to do, our best chance to win the World Series, and Durocher did it. He wasn't thinking about history; he was thinking about winning.

I never even thought about it being an all–African American outfield. I wasn't brought up to think that way. Somebody had to mention it to me before I realized it.

No discussion of Negro Leagues third basemen would be complete without mention of Howard Easterling, a terrific player in the 1930s and 1940s for the Cincinnati Tigers, Chicago American Giants, Homestead Grays, and New York Cubans.

Just a little guy, 5'9" tall and 175 pounds, Howard was such a powerful switch-hitter that the Grays batted him fifth behind Buck Leonard and Josh Gibson when they won consecutive Negro National League pennants from 1940 through 1943. In 1941 he was 6–10 in the Homestead's doubleheader sweep of the New York Cubans in the league championship series. The following year, he batted .333 in the Negro Leagues World Series. Easterling was the East's starting third baseman in the 1940, 1944, 1946, and 1949 Negro Leagues All-Star Games.

In the spring of 1943, three years before the Dodgers signed Jackie Robinson, Clarence "Pants" Rowland, president of the Pacific Coast League, announced that three Negro Leagues players—Chet Brewer, Nate Moreland, and Easterling—would be given trials with teams in his league. Two weeks later, presumably under pressure from team owners, Rowland reneged on the promise, and Easterling never got his chance to play in a white man's league.

Career Summaries

Third Baseman	Years	Teams
Ray Dandridge *Hit in a record 32 consecutive games in outlaw Mexican League in 1948*	1933–49	Detroit Stars, Nashville Elite Giants, Newark Dodgers, Newark Eagles, New York Cubans
Judy Johnson *Batted .339 in six seasons in the Cuban Winter League from 1923 to 1930*	1918–36	Atlantic City Bacharach Giants, Hilldale Daisies, Homestead Grays, Darby Daisies, Pittsburgh Crawfords
Oliver Marcelle *Collected 12 hits in 1926 Negro Leagues World Series*	1918–32	Brooklyn Royal Giants, Atlantic City Bacharach Giants, Lincoln Giants, Detroit Stars, Baltimore Black Sox
Jud Wilson *Hit .435 in six career East-West All-Star Games*	1922–45	Baltimore Black Sox, Homestead Grays, Philadelphia Stars, Pittsburgh Crawfords
Henry Thompson *Led Negro American League with 20 stolen bases in 1948*	1943–48	Kansas City Monarchs

SIX

Left Fielder

Neil Robinson was one of those unheralded players who never got the recognition he deserved; he just played hard and played well, mostly for the Memphis Red Sox, and he was their drawing card—a crowd-pleaser. He was a really good hitter and a good outfielder, and he could steal bases. He was something like Artie Wilson; he didn't pull the ball very much, so pitchers pitched him inside.

You just have to look at Robinson's record in All-Star Games to appreciate him. In eight All-Star Games, he batted .476. Playing for the West squad in the 1939 All-Star Game, he had three of his side's eight hits. He wasn't flashy, and he didn't have the reputation that some of the better-known players like Josh Gibson, Cool Papa Bell, Buck Leonard, and a lot of others had, so he was bypassed when it came to the Hall of Fame. But he was a really good, steady ballplayer: a terrific hitter and a good all-around player.

1. NEIL ROBINSON

2. MINNIE MINOSO

3. VIC HARRIS

4. SANDY AMOROS

5. WILLARD BROWN

Neil played 15 seasons in the Negro Leagues and had a lifetime average of .303. Marlin Carter, his teammate with Memphis and the Cincinnati Tigers, said Robinson was "about the most valuable player we had on the southern

Neil Robinson wasn't flashy and never seemed to get the recognition he deserved, but he batted over .300 during a 15-year career in the Negro Leagues. *Photo courtesy of the Rucker Archive.*

teams. He didn't do anything flashy; he just got the job done day after day. He was the kind of player you counted on."

And Winfield Welch, who managed the Birmingham Black Barons, called Neil "the kind of player you build a team around."

Playing for the Tigers, Robinson once hit a ball so far in Cincinnati's West End Park that the city changed the name of the park from West End to Neil Robinson Park.

It baffles me that Neil has never even been mentioned as a Hall of Fame candidate. I personally think he belongs, but for him to not even get nominated is a mystery to me.

Red Parnell of the Philadelphia Stars, a great team player, is another outfielder that is mostly overlooked. Red did get nominated in the last Hall of Fame election. He didn't make it, but he at least got his due by being placed on the ballot—Neil Robinson didn't even get that honor.

It's one of the great names in the history of baseball—for both the Negro Leagues and the major leagues—Saturnino Orestes Armas (Arrieta) Minoso, the lovable, ageless Cuban-Minnie.

Minnie Minoso broke into the Negro Leagues with the New York Cubans in 1946 as a third baseman. After three years with the Cubans, Minoso signed with the Cleveland Indians and played in nine games for them in 1949. He spent the next year in the minor leagues and was brought back in 1951.

The '51 season was just a couple of weeks old when Minnie was part of a three-team trade that sent him to Chicago, where he became the first black player to wear a White Sox uniform. He would also become one of the most popular players ever to wear a White Sox uniform because of his flamboyant, all-out style of play; his daring, dashing base running; his good nature; and his wonderful sense of humor.

Minnie was an instant hit in Chicago. In his first at-bat for the White Sox, he hit a home run against the Yankees in the first inning. Five innings later, a Yankees rookie also hit his first major league home run. His name was Mickey Mantle.

Minoso finished the 1951 season (he was still considered a rookie) with a .326 average (second in the American League), 10 home runs, 76 RBIs, and a league-leading 31 stolen bases. Gil McDougald of the Yankees, who batted .306 with 14 home runs, 63 RBIs, and 14 stolen bases, was voted the Rookie of the Year in the American League.

Soon Minoso was one of the best players in the American League. He led the league in steals in 1952 and 1953 and in triples in 1954, and he tied for the league lead in doubles in 1957. He was fearless at the plate, a guy who would do anything to get on base. During his career, he was hit by 189 pitches, an American League record that was later broken by Don Baylor.

After the '57 season, Minnie bounced around: back to Cleveland for two years, the White Sox for two more, then to the Cardinals and the Senators, and back to the White Sox in 1964, after which he retired at the age of 43 with a lifetime batting average of .298, eight .300 seasons, and seven All-Star selections.

When master showman Bill Veeck, who had great affection and respect for Minoso, returned as owner of the White Sox, he brought Minnie out of retirement late in the 1976 season. In his second game, Minoso got his final major league hit and became the oldest player to get a base hit in the major leagues. He was two months short of his 54th birthday.

Minnie Minoso left the Negro Leagues to join the Cleveland Indians, who then traded him to the Chicago White Sox, where he blossomed into a huge star.

In 1980 Minoso was again put on the White Sox's active roster, this time so he could join Nick Altrock as one of only two players to appear in a major league game in five different decades. Minoso batted twice as a designated hitter without a hit and then retired once more. Or did he?

In 1991 the Miami Miracle of the Florida State League wanted to sign Minoso, but Commissioner Fay Vincent denied the request.

Undaunted, Minoso surfaced two years later as designated hitter for the St. Paul Saints of the Independent Northern League. Minoso, seven months past his 70th birthday, grounded back to the pitcher in what would be the final at-bat of a fabulous and colorful career.

Vic Harris was a Punch-and-Judy hitter, but you couldn't get the son of a gun out. He was a lot like my old New York Giants teammate Artie Wilson, a left-handed hitter who hit everything to left field. When we played him, we'd pinch the corner outfielders against him, with the left fielder near the line, the center fielder in left-center, and the right fielder in right-center. He could hit, and he'd get on base somehow. And he was mean, so mean that he was called "Vicious" Vic—of course, that name also had something to do with his aggressive style of play. He'd spike you and do anything to win.

I was playing shortstop for the Eagles one day, and I had the ball, waiting to tag Harris out at second base. He came into second with a jump, and he cut my leg. I said, "If you ever do that again, Vic, I'll take this damn ball and break your neck. You understand?" He said, "Get your damn foot out of the way."

Vic Harris was so mean that he had the nickname "Vicious Vic," but when I had my chance to really retaliate after a hard slide into second base, I backed off. *Photo courtesy of the Rucker Archive.*

Near the end of the season, there was the same kind of play. Harris was on first base, and a ground ball was hit to the second baseman, Larry Doby, who fed me the ball at the bag. It was my chance to get even with that SOB. I took the throw and drew back; Harris's head was right there in front of me. If I had thrown the ball, I'da hit him right in the head, and I might have killed him. I wasn't worried about throwing the ball to first; all I wanted to do was just throw it toward first, but I wanted to hit him in the head first. But at the last second, I couldn't do it. I couldn't kill this man, so I let him go.

About 25 years later, Vic was living in Pacoima, California, outside of Los Angeles, and I went to his house for a visit. He said, "Monte, thanks for not killing me on that play at second base."

Vic was a rarity in the Negro Leagues, a guy who spent 23 years of his 28-year career as a player and manager with one team, the Homestead Grays, as a player and later as manager during their glory days.

Most baseball fans know the name **Sandy Amoros** because of one catch he made in Game 7 of the 1955 World Series, but those of us who played, or followed, Negro Leagues baseball know Edmundo Isasi Amoros not as a defensive replacement but as a speedy, slap-hitting little outfielder from Cuba. Sandy arrived in the United States just as the Negro Leagues were beginning to decline because so many players were signing with major league clubs. In his only season with the New York Cubans of the Negro American League he batted .338.

The Dodgers signed him, farmed him out, and then brought him to Brooklyn for 20 games in 1952. They farmed him out again the next year and then brought him back in 1954.

Sandy spent the next four years with the Dodgers in Brooklyn, went back to the minor leagues in 1958, and rejoined the Dodgers in Los Angeles in 1959. The following season, he was traded to Detroit, where he finished out his career.

Sandy spoke hardly any English, but he had this bubbly personality and always had a smile on his face. He was well liked by everyone.

In his seven years in the majors, Amoros was never more than a platoon player, pinch-hitter, pinch runner, and defensive replacement. He never batted higher than .277 in any season, never hit more than 16 home runs, or

Sandy Amoros batted .338 in his only season with the New York Cubans, and his major league career wasn't particularly spectacular, except for a World Series–saving catch for the Brooklyn Dodgers in 1955.

drove in more than 58 runs, so you would have to say his major league career was mediocre—except for one day in October 1955.

It was one of the most memorable moments in World Series history.

The Dodgers and Yankees were tied, three games apiece, when they met in Yankee Stadium on October 4. The Dodgers, who had never won a World Series in Brooklyn and who had lost to the Yankees in the World Series four times in the previous eight years, held a 2–0 lead going into the bottom of the sixth with rookie Johnny Podres on the mound and pitching a gem. He had allowed just three hits over the first five innings.

Jim Gilliam had started the game in left field, and Don Zimmer was at second base. But when the Dodgers scored their second run in the top of the sixth, manager Walter Alston made a couple of moves to shore up his defense for the final four innings. He brought Gilliam in to replace Zimmer at second and put Amoros in left field in Gilliam's place. The moves didn't come a moment too soon.

Podres walked Billy Martin leading off the bottom of the sixth, and Gil McDougald dropped a bunt along the third-base line and beat it out for a hit. With Yogi Berra due up, it appeared the Yankees were primed for a big rally that would frustrate the Dodgers once again.

Berra reached for an outside pitch and lofted a high, twisting fly down the left-field line that looked like it might reach the seats or, at worst, drop inside the line for extra bases. That's when Amoros went into his Houdini act.

A couple of things to point out about the play: the Dodgers' outfield was pulled over to the right against Berra—a dead pull hitter—with left fielder Amoros playing practically in center field. So Sandy had to run a country mile to catch up with Berra's drive.

Would Gilliam, who was fast but a step or two slower than the speedy Amoros, have been able to catch up with the ball? Most experts say it is doubtful.

The second thing to bear in mind is that Gilliam was a right-handed thrower, so he wore his glove on his left hand; Amoros was a left-handed thrower and wore his glove on his right hand, which meant that he was about a foot closer to the ball that Berra hit than Gilliam would have been.

Amoros sprinted toward the left-field corner, and he and the ball reached the barrier at exactly the same time. In a dead sprint, Sandy stuck out his right hand, and the ball settled right in his glove. The consensus is that there is no way Gilliam would have made that catch.

And that wasn't the end of the play. After he caught the ball, Amoros spun around and, in one motion, fired the ball to shortstop Pee Wee Reese, who had ranged out to left field as the cutoff man. Amoros's throw hit Reese chest-high. Pee Wee wheeled and relayed the ball to Gil Hodges at first to double up McDougald. Podres then retired Hank Bauer on a ground ball to short to preserve the Dodgers' two-run lead.

Podres pitched around a single by Elston Howard in the seventh and singles by Phil Rizzuto and McDougald in the eighth and then retired the Yankees in order in the ninth, and Brooklyn had won its first World Series.

Podres was the World Series Most Valuable Player for his shutout in Game 7, but the world knows he never would have done it without Amoros's fantastic catch and his one big moment in baseball history.

Ask 100 people who played or managed in the Negro Leagues or who watched or were historians of Negro Leagues baseball to name the best left fielder in the league, and 99 of them will tell you that Monte Irvin deserves to be the left fielder on the all–Negro Leagues team—no contest. The one dissenter would be Irvin, who is too modest, too self-effacing, too classy to select himself on his all-time Negro Leagues team. So let others say it for him.

Cool Papa Bell: "Most of the black ballplayers thought Monte Irvin should have been the first black in the major leagues. Monte was our best young ballplayer at the time. He could do everything. You see, we wanted men who could go there and hit the ball over the fence, and Monte could do that. He could hit that long ball, he had a great arm, he could field, [and] he could run. Yes, he could do everything. It's not that Jackie Robinson wasn't a good ballplayer, but we wanted Monte because we knew what he could do."

Roy Campanella: "He was the best all-around player I ever saw."

Jimmy Powers: "You talk about Joe DiMaggio; you ought to see Monte Irvin play center field and throw."

Sports columnist Jimmy Powers wrote the above in the *New York Daily News* in 1941, six years before Jackie Robinson broke in with the Brooklyn Dodgers. Powers was a longtime advocate of Negro Leagues baseball and campaigned for blacks to get their chance in the major leagues long before it was fashionable.

Bobby Thomson: "I had as much respect for Monte as anybody I ever played with, as a player and as a man. I was impressed with him from the first time I saw him. The build he had—he was built like a panther. Strong. All muscle. He could run; he could hit and hit for power. He could do every-thing. We all respected him. Anybody who knew him respected him. He was a quiet, nice guy, soft-spoken and polite: a true gentleman. After the 1951 season, I enjoyed going out on speaking engagements with Monte because I liked his company and it gave me the chance to give him the recognition he deserved. I got a lot of pleasure out of saying, 'Yeah, I'm the guy that hit the home run, but without this guy, we wouldn't have been there at the end.' And I meant it. He was the reason we had a chance to beat the Dodgers."

Effa Manley: "Monte was the choice of all Negro National and American League club owners to serve as the number one player to join a white major league team. We all agreed in meetings: he was the best qualified by temperament, character, ability, sense of loyalty, morals, age, experience, and physique to represent us as the first black player to enter the white majors since the Walker brothers [Moses and Welday] back in the late 1880s. Of course, Branch Rickey lifted Jackie Robinson of the Negro ball and made him the first, and it turned out fine."

Although it is true that Irvin played more games for the Newark Eagles at shortstop and in center field than he did in left field, when he got his chance to play in the major leagues, he made his mark with the New York Giants as a left fielder and, therefore, would rank as the number one left fielder in Negro Leagues history.

Best estimates put his 11-year Negro Leagues average at .350. He won the Negro National League batting title in 1941 with an average of .395, and in 1946, after returning from the army, he won the batting title again with a .394 average and then batted .462 with three home runs to lead the Eagles over the Kansas City Monarchs in the Negro Leagues World Series, four games to three.

Irvin joined the New York Giants in 1949 and soon became a local hero and a household name. But he was already a hero in his own household, according to younger brother Milton of Chatham, New Jersey:

Monte was a great young man, family oriented and very protective of his younger siblings. He was very helpful around the house, and he always had a job after school and during the summer. He worked in a bowling alley, and he caddied on the local golf course.

He was very popular in school. He had a strong, athletic body and great ability in four sports [in addition to baseball, football, and basketball, Irvin set the New Jersey state record in the javelin]. Everybody loved him, his classmates and his teachers. He was a good student, and I remember that he had beautiful penmanship. Coming after him in school was a problem for his younger brothers, me and my brother Calvin, because Monte set such a high standard on the athletic field and in the classroom that we were expected to live up to him, but we couldn't.

Monte Irvin: "I have been very lucky. You have to be lucky to live a long and full life, as I have. I have tried to live by the golden rule: to treat others the way you want to be treated. When you do that, it comes back to you in so many ways."

Willard Brown's only weakness as a ballplayer was bad timing. Don't judge him by what he did in the major leagues; his record there does him a great disservice.

In July 1947 the St. Louis Browns purchased the contracts of Brown and Henry Thompson from the Kansas City Monarchs, making them the third and fourth African Americans to play in the major leagues.

Neither of them did well with the Browns, and they were both quickly released, Thompson after 27 games, Brown after 21. Thompson got a second chance and made good on it, with eight productive seasons for the New York Giants. Unfortunately, Brown never got a second chance.

Willard did make history by becoming the first African American to hit a home run in the American League, but that was his only home run. In 21 games, he batted just .179, and then St. Louis let him go.

I can only conjecture as to why Brown, who was such a force in the Negro Leagues, helping the Monarchs win six pennants between 1937 and 1946 and making the All-Star team eight times, failed in the major leagues when others with less talent than he had succeeded. Perhaps it was the pressure of making history and playing in the majors' southernmost city. Whatever the case, I know he was better than his major league record indicates.

It wasn't that he was too old—just 31, supposedly at the peak of his ability—when the call came, and when he washed out in St. Louis, he continued to put up big numbers in the minor leagues, the Negro Leagues, and the Puerto Rican Winter League.

When he was released by the Browns, Willard returned to the Monarchs and batted .374 with 18 home runs. After the Negro Leagues season, he went to Puerto Rico, hit 27 home runs, and won the Puerto Rican Winter League triple crown, and then he did it again two years later. In Puerto Rico he was so highly regarded that the natives called him *Esse Hombre* ("That Man").

In 1951 he won the Negro American League batting title with a .417 average and finished his career with five seasons in the minor leagues. In 1954 he

Willard Brown just didn't make the transition to the major leagues in his only chance, but he will always be a Negro Leagues legend and was inducted into the Baseball Hall of Fame in 2006.

hit 35 home runs in the Texas League, but it was too late for a second chance in the majors. He was 38 years old by then.

Known for using a 40-ounce bat, Brown had a lifetime batting average of .355 in the Negro Leagues and was such a lethal power hitter that Josh Gibson referred to him as "Home Run" Brown. Despite his failure in the major leagues, Brown's greatness in the Negro Leagues was validated when he was elected to the Hall of Fame in 2006, 10 years after his death.

Career Summaries

Left Fielder	Years	Teams
Neil Robinson *Had 10 hits (.476) in eight East-West All-Star Game appearances*	1935–52	Cincinnati Tigers, Homestead Grays, Memphis Red Sox
Minnie Minoso *Had identical .294 average in Negro National League and Cuban Winter League in 1946*	1945–48	New York Cubans
Vic Harris *Played in 1938, 1942, 1943, and 1947 East-West All-Star Games*	1923–45	Toledo Tigers, Cleveland Tate Stars, Cleveland Browns, Chicago American Giants, Homestead Grays, Pittsburgh Crawfords, Baltimore Elite Giants, Birmingham Black Barons, Detroit Wolves
Sandy Amoros *In 1953, hit .373 in Cuban Winter League*	1950	New York Cubans
Willard Brown *Negro American League batting and home-run champion in both 1937 and 1938*	1935–52, 1958	Kansas City Monarchs

SEVEN

Center Fielder

The first time I ever set eyes on **Willie Mays** was when he joined the New York Giants in May 1951, but I had certainly heard a lot about him by then.

Even though I was gone from the Negro Leagues in 1948, I kept hearing about this spectacular 17-year-old center fielder from Alabama who was playing for the Birmingham Black Barons and making a name for himself. Later, when the Giants signed him, I continued to hear about him tearing up the Double A Interstate League with Trenton and then the Triple A American Association with Minneapolis.

Leo Durocher kept talking about this youngster in Minneapolis that could do it all. Mays was hitting a sizzling .477 in 35 games for Minneapolis when the Giants called him up, and you could tell immediately how great he was. I didn't know he was going to become the great home-run hitter that he became, but you could see the way he handled himself—catch the ball, throw the ball, run like crazy—that he was something special.

1. WILLIE MAYS

2. OSCAR CHARLESTON

3. COOL PAPA BELL

4. LARRY DOBY

5. TURKEY STEARNES

You saw that talent right away, in his first series against the Phillies in Philadelphia. He caught everything that was hit and threw out everybody that ran. He was disappointed that he didn't get any hits, but Durocher told him, "Listen, Willie, let me tell you this. Don't you worry about hitting. Your hitting will come. Just go out and play the way you've been playing. You're my center fielder every day, don't you worry about it."

Durocher was good that way, a master psychologist. You might not like him as a person—and a lot of people didn't, including some of his players—but on the field, you couldn't beat him as a manager.

Allow me to digress here a while to give you some insight into the machinations of Leo Durocher, who was an important figure not only in Mays's career but in mine as well. Generally, I got along with Durocher just fine, but we had our differences at times. Leo used to say, "I like to get on you in the clubhouse, but after the game is over, tomorrow is a new day with me. I don't hold any grudges." And he didn't. Whatever he did, it usually worked.

One time we were sitting on an airplane, and we had this thing going on where a guy would hit you and you were supposed to pass it along. I was sitting next to Durocher, and he started hitting too hard. I said, "Leo, do you really mean it, or are you just playing? Remember what I did to Seminick [earlier that season, I had bowled over Andy Seminick, the catcher for the Phillies, and leveled him in a collision at home plate]? If you really mean it, I'm going to have to treat you the way I did Seminick."

Durocher would get on me sometimes. "You're not swinging the bat the way you can," he would say, and I told him, "That stuff doesn't work with me, understand. I'm doing the best I can." And so he dropped it.

In the tenth inning of the first game of the 1954 World Series against Cleveland, Durocher took me out and put Dusty Rhodes up to hit for me, and Dusty hit a three-run home run off Bob Lemon to win the game.

In the second game, Leo did it again. He put Rhodes up to hit for me in the fifth inning, and Dusty singled to drive in a run. Third game, the same thing. Rhodes batted for me in the third inning and singled to drive in two runs.

I knew what Durocher was doing; he was playing the hot hand. But I didn't like it, and Leo knew it.

By the fourth game I thought Durocher might start Dusty, but he didn't. I looked at the lineup card and I was in there, and I got a single in the fifth inning off Hal Newhouser that drove in two runs and broke the game open. We ended up winning, 7–4, and swept the Indians in four games.

That winter I saw Durocher, and he was kind of timid about coming over to say hello. He thought I was going to beat him up.

"No, Leo," I said. "I never had any thoughts like that, but tell me this: Dusty was pinch hitting and winning games, why did you start me in that fourth game?"

He said, "I knew my man had to come through sooner or later."

Yeah, Leo, bull!

But that was Leo. He knew how to get the most out of his players, and he knew how to handle Mays when he was a rookie and wasn't hitting. He

Willie Mays, shown sliding into home, was just a 17-year-old when he played for the Birmingham Black Barons, but it didn't take long for the major league Giants to snatch up the phenom and launch one of the most prolific careers in the history of the game.

would say the right thing to Willie at the right time, and he would phrase it just right. He handled Willie perfectly. Durocher loved Willie, and Willie loved Durocher.

Mays went hitless in his first 12 at-bats, and then he got his first hit, a home run off Warren Spahn, the first of his 660 home runs. He went hitless in his next 13 at-bats, but Durocher stayed with him, and as Leo predicted, the hits started to come. Willie finished with a .274 average, 20 home runs, and 68 runs batted in and was voted National League Rookie of the Year. He was the missing piece of the puzzle that enabled us to catch the Dodgers and win the pennant.

Bobby Thomson had been playing center field, but when Willie got there, Durocher moved Bobby to third base to fill that hole. Thomson batted .293 that season, drove in 101 runs, and hit 32 home runs, including the one everybody knows about, the shot heard 'round the world, that beat the Dodgers in the third game of the playoffs.

Those two moves—Mays in center field and Thomson to third base—were the making of our team. Bobby was a really good center fielder. He could run everything down in the outfield, but even though he had a good arm, for some reason he never did throw anybody out. When Mays took over in center field, he started throwing out runners going from first to third and from second to home and making sensational catches really easily, so we knew we had a diamond in the rough. All they had to do was polish him up a little bit.

When Willie joined us, Durocher assigned him to room with me on the road. I had an immediate kinship with Mays, possibly because we were both born in Alabama. He was just a baby, 20 years old. I was 12 years older than Willie, and I had been around a while, so I kind of took him under my wing and treated him like a kid brother. I told him what to do, what not to do, who to talk to, who not to talk to, what this pitcher's best pitch was, what to look for—that sort of thing. I kind of looked out for him, was somebody he could talk to because we had been through a lot of the same things.

Mays had been discriminated against in the minor leagues. I told him, "Don't worry about that; forget all that stuff. Now you're where you want to be. This is where you want to succeed. This is the place to play. You're young; you've got all this talent. Have no anger. Just show up every day, go out, and give your best." And he did. He was such a great player from the start, and he loved to play the game. He played it with a flair—the basket catches, his cap flying off when he ran, his aggressiveness in the field and on the bases. He went all out all the time. He was a joy to watch.

Mays had this high-pitched voice, like a little kid, and once he got comfortable, he would talk all the time to anybody. When he talked to people, he had this habit of starting out by saying, "Say, hey," and that's how he came to be called "the Say Hey Kid." The newspaper writers and photographers loved him for his boyish exuberance and his friendly good nature.

Willie Mays loved to play the game. He played it with a flair—the basket catches, his cap flying off when he ran, his aggressiveness in the field and on the bases. He went all out all the time.

Because he was still just a kid himself, Willie liked to play stickball in the streets of Harlem with the neighborhood kids. Photographers heard about it, and they went up to Harlem to take pictures of Mays, the Giants center fielder, swinging a stickball bat.

It was this boyishness that was Mays's charm and that set him apart from other great players.

That first year, I showed Willie around the league a little bit. By his second year, he was such a big star and a fan favorite that he was showing me around the league.

I have often been asked who was better, Willie Mays or Joe DiMaggio.

DiMaggio was my idol as a kid, and let me just say this, you can't get any better as a center fielder than Joe DiMaggio was, and Mays patterned himself after DiMaggio. DiMaggio was Mays's hero. Joe was a leader. He demanded excellence of himself, and he earned the respect of everyone by the way he carried himself, the way he caught the ball, and the way he threw the ball.

Once at an old-timers game in Dallas, somebody asked Durocher who was better, Mays or DiMaggio.

"It's paper thin," Durocher said, "but I have to pick Mays because every day, 154 games, he's going to be ready to play 154 times. You just have to write his name in the lineup."

DiMaggio was sitting right there, and he heard all this. I said to Leo, "Joe's not going to like what you just said," and, sure enough, DiMaggio stopped speaking to Durocher.

The bottom line is you can't go wrong with either one. They're number one and number one(a) as far as I'm concerned. Willie hit more home runs and stole more bases, but Joe was a better hitter. Willie would go through streaks where for a week or so he wouldn't make good contact and he'd strike out a lot and look kind of silly. And then he'd straighten himself out and the home runs would come in bunches.

Willie could look bad at times, but I never saw Joe look bad. He didn't strike out often (only 369 strikeouts in 6,821 at-bats; Mays struck out 1,526 times in 10,881 at-bats), and even when DiMaggio did strike out, he didn't look bad doing it. Do you know how good you have to be to have a 56-game hitting streak like DiMaggio had? He got a few breaks here and there, but to do that day in and day out, week in and week out—that's one record that I believe will never be broken.

As a fielder, I'd give Willie a slight edge over DiMaggio. To me, the difference between them was a matter of style. Willie did things that could pull you out of your seat. He played with great emotion. Joe didn't. The only time he showed any emotion on a baseball field was when Al Gionfriddo robbed him of a home run in the 1947 World Series and Joe kicked at the dirt in frustration as he rounded first base.

Willie was spectacular. Joe made all of the plays with style and grace, but he was too reserved to dive after a ball. Joe got such a great jump on a ball that he always seemed to be there to make the catch without having to leave his feet. I told that to Willie, and he said, "If he didn't dive once in a while, there must have been balls he should have caught."

There were very few balls Mays could have caught but didn't. Maybe none. People talk about the catch he made with his back to home plate in the Polo Grounds against Vic Wertz in the eighth inning of the first game of the 1954 World Series. As the left fielder in that game playing alongside Willie, I had a bird's-eye view of that catch, and it was something special. It got a lot of attention because it came with two men on base and nobody out in the eighth inning of an important tie game in front of a national audience, but Willie said it wasn't his best catch.

He said his best catch was one he made against Dodger Bobby Morgan in Ebbets Field. The bases were loaded, and Morgan hit a shot that was headed for the wall in left-center. Mays took off, and on a dead run, he caught the ball just as it was about to smash into the wall. Then he crashed into the wall, fell to the ground, and rolled over. He appeared to have knocked himself out momentarily, but he still held on to the ball. The ball was in his glove, and his eyes were closed. He lay there for a few seconds, and Durocher almost had a heart attack. Leo raced out to center field to see if Mays was all right.

"Willie, Willie," Leo shouted in fear.

Mays slowly opened his eyes and looked up at Leo with a smile on his face.

"What are you doing?" Durocher said. "You scared me half to death."

"I was just taking a little rest," Mays said.

That was Willie. He never lost that little boy's demeanor.

In the spring of 1952, the year after we won the National League pennant, we were playing an exhibition game against the Cleveland Indians. I slid into third base and heard a pop. I had broken my ankle. I lay on the ground, writhing in excruciating pain. Mays had rushed over, and he looked down at me, tears in his eyes.

"Why are you crying?" I said. "I'm the one who's hurt."

"I know," Willie said in that high-pitched voice, "but we just lost our chance to win the World Series."

Oscar Charleston was the Willie Mays of his day, the 1920s and 1930s, meaning he was the Negro Leagues' best center fielder and a great all-around player.

Many people say Charleston was the greatest ever to play in the Negro Leagues, hitting, fielding, throwing, running, hitting for power; they say Oscar was "the man."

I saw Oscar play only one time, in an exhibition game late in his career when he had moved to first base, but they tell me he was something else as a center fielder. He was a crowd-pleaser. Between games of doubleheaders, he would put on throwing exhibitions. He'd stand in center field and somebody would hit him fly balls and Charleston would throw strikes to home plate on a fly.

Oscar was built like Babe Ruth, a left-handed hitter with a barrel chest and spindly legs, but he could run. They called him "the black Ty Cobb" because he was a swashbuckler, very aggressive, fearless, and ruthless on the bases. He slid hard into bases, spikes high, and would do anything to win, even cut a fielder if necessary, just like Cobb did. But he was said to be a better fielder and to have more power than Cobb.

"Charleston could hit that ball a mile," said Dizzy Dean, who pitched against him in barnstorming games. "He didn't have a weakness. When he came up, we just threw it and hoped like hell he wouldn't get a hold of one and send it out of the park."

As a fielder, he was compared to Tris Speaker, who was the standard for major league center fielders in his day.

Dave Malarcher, who played right field alongside Charleston once said, "Some people asked me, 'Why are you playing so close to the right-field line?' What they didn't know was that Charleston covered all three fields and my responsibility was to make sure I got any ball down the line and those in foul territory."

Oscar was born in Indianapolis in 1896. At the age of 14, he left home to join the U.S. Army. Stationed in the Philippines, he played baseball and ran track for the Negro 24th Infantry, once running the 220-yard dash in 23 seconds. After the army, he returned home and joined the Indianapolis ABCs, with whom he had been a batboy in his youth. He was a star player, but it wasn't long before his pugnacious side surfaced.

As a rookie, he got into a fight with an umpire and was held on $1,000 bond and suspended from the team. Repentant, he wrote a public apology to the fans.

"The fact is that I could not overcome my temper as often times a baseball player cannot," he wrote. "I consider the incident highly unwise."

His greatest year was 1921, when Charleston led the Negro National League in hitting with a .445 batting average, triples with 10, home runs with 14, and stolen bases with 28 in 50 games. Later he played with the Homestead Grays, teaming with such stars as Josh Gibson, "Smokey" Joe Williams, and Judy Johnson, and then with the Pittsburgh Crawfords. Aging and getting heavy, Oscar finished out his playing career as a first baseman.

When his playing days were at an end, Charleston became manager of the Crawfords. As a manager, he was tough and demanding and just as pugnacious as he was as a player. There are stories of his temper flaring and of fights with opposing players, umpires, owners, and scouts, and there is even one in which he confronted a member of the Ku Klux Klan, ripped off his hood, and dared him to speak.

Jimmie Crutchfield tells the following story of an aging Charleston, as reported by Robert Peterson in *Only the Ball Was White,* his wonderful book on Negro Leagues baseball:

We were playing a major league All-Star team one night in Des Moines, Iowa—Bob Feller, Gus Suhr, Ival Goodman, Al Todd, Jimmy King, Big Jim Weaver, Johnny Mize, Jim Winford—oh, they had a heckuva club! Now this was in 1936 when Charleston was big and fat. I heard him on the bench saying, "I just don't get a thrill out of batting anymore unless there's someone on the bases."

Oscar Charleston was considered to be the Willie Mays of his time in the Negro Leagues—he had all the tools and exceptional all-around talent.

He had popped up a couple of times. Sure enough, we got two men on against Big Jim Weaver, and Charleston said, "Now this is what I've been waiting for." And he doubled against the left-center-field wall and waddled into second base. That's the kind of guy Charleston was. If I had to pick the best player I saw in my time, it would be hard to pick between Charleston and Josh Gibson. When the chips were down and you needed somebody to bat in the clutch, even at his age, Charleston was as good as anybody playing baseball.

Integration in the major leagues came too late for Oscar Charleston. By 1946 he was well past his prime. But he was held in such high esteem as a baseball man that Branch Rickey hired him to scout the Negro Leagues for talent, and Oscar was instrumental in Rickey's signing of Jackie Robinson.

*J*Preston "Pete" Hill was an anachronism, a 1950s- and 1960s-style player who was stuck in the 1910s and 1920s, the so-called dead-ball era. Hill was also the first great outfielder in Negro Leagues baseball.

He had incredible range in the field and a howitzer for a throwing arm and was a terror on the base paths.

As a hitter, Hill was peerless in his time, a slashing left-handed batter equally adept at hitting left-handed and right-handed pitchers and who sprayed line drives to all fields and had an unerring eye for the strike zone. Cum Posey, owner of the Homestead Grays, called Hill "the most consistent hitter of his lifetime."

Although at 6'1" and 215 pounds he had the size and strength to hit balls out of the park, that was not his style, or the style of the day. He was more of a contact hitter who often led his league in triples. In a four-year stretch from 1910 to 1913, Hill batted .423, .400, .357, and .302, a cumulative average of .371. Later he was a successful manager for the Detroit Stars and Baltimore Black Sox.

It has been said that if one were to pick an all-star team from the dead-ball era, the outfield would consist of Ty Cobb, Tris Speaker, and Pete Hill, with Hill playing center field.

Anybody who ever saw him play said **Cool Papa Bell** was the fastest thing in spiked shoes. When I got to the Newark Eagles, Bell was on his way out. He might have been around at the time, but he wasn't playing very much by then. But they say that in his day, he was something to behold—a switch-hitter, a base stealer, and a great center fielder who could outrun the ball. Nobody could run with Cool Papa, so much so that there are all kinds of stories about his speed—some real, some contrived—like the following one from Josh Gibson: "Cool Papa Bell was so fast he could get out of bed, turn out the lights across the room and be back in bed under the covers before the room was dark."

Other far-fetched stories were that he once hit a ball through the pitcher's mound and it hit him as he slid into second and that he once stole two bases on one pitch.

More believable is the story that in an exhibition game against major leaguers, Bell was on first base when Satchel Paige put down a bunt. As Cleveland Indians catcher Roy Partee picked up the ball and was about to throw to first base, Cool Papa brushed by him to score. There's another story that claims Bell often went from first to third on a sacrifice bunt and that he once scored from first on a bunt when he saw that nobody was covering the plate.

Jimmie Crutchfield said that when Bell hit a ball back to the pitcher "everybody would yell, 'Hurry,'" and Judy Johnson said that when Cool Papa came to bat with the bases empty, the infielders moved in as if there were a man on third. "You couldn't play back in your regular position or you'd never throw him out," Judy said.

According to Satchel Paige, "If Cool Papa had known about colleges, or if colleges had known about Papa, Jesse Owens would have looked like he was walking."

Cool Papa Bell, his blazing speed the stuff of legend, is one of the most enduring figures from the Negro Leagues.

Owens, the great Olympic champion sprinter once accepted a challenge to race George Case, the Washington Senators outfielder who was considered the fastest man in the major leagues in the 1940s. Several times, Owens was issued a challenge to race against Cool Papa, and he always declined.

Because of his ability to get on base by slapping the ball around when batting either left-handed or right-handed, his ability to run down fly balls in the outfield, and his catchy nickname and blinding speed, Bell is one of the most enduring characters ever to play in the Negro Leagues. He is said to have stolen 175 bases in one 200-game season, and he was a great center fielder with one weakness: he didn't have Willie Mays's arm. He came up as a pitcher and hurt his arm. As a result, he couldn't throw a lick. But he didn't have to. He played very shallow, and he could outrun any ball that was hit.

Just like Oscar Charleston before him, Papa's best years came before integration in the major leagues. But Bell did get an offer from a big-league club. It came from the St. Louis Browns in 1951, five years after he had retired from baseball. He was 48 years old at the time.

Bell declined the offer and returned to his job as a custodian and night watchman at St. Louis's city hall.

It was **Larry Doby**'s lot in life to be overlooked. Always a bridesmaid, never a bride! He arrived with the Cleveland Indians in August 1947, four months after Jackie Robinson started with the Brooklyn Dodgers, and was overshadowed by Jackie.

The second person to do something historic is rarely celebrated. John Adams was overshadowed by George Washington; Buzz Aldrin, the second man to walk on the moon, was obscured by Neil Armstrong. I know that Roger Bannister was the first man to break the four-minute-mile barrier and that Charles Lindbergh was the first man to fly solo across the Atlantic Ocean, but I can't tell you who the second four-minute miler or the second transcontinental pilot was.

The fact is, Doby was a pioneer in his own right, and he did achieve several historic baseball firsts. He was the first African American to play in the American League, to lead his league in home runs (1952), to hit a home run in the World Series, and to win a World Series (1948).

It's also a fact that Larry suffered the same indignities, the same prejudice, and the same loneliness with the Indians as Jackie did with the Dodgers.

Larry Doby's greatness was somewhat overshadowed by Jackie Robinson's timing. Few people remember that although he was the second black player in the major leagues he was the first to win a World Series and the first to lead his league in home runs.

"The only difference," he once said, "was that Jackie Robinson got all the publicity. You didn't hear much about what I was going through, because the media didn't want to repeat the same story. I couldn't react to situations from a physical standpoint. My reaction was to hit the ball as far as I could."

Larry told me that when he joined the Indians, the manager, Lou Boudreau, called the team together, lined up all the players, and introduced each one of them to Doby. Three of them refused to shake Larry's hand. Before long Indians owner Bill Veeck got rid of all three.

Knowing Doby—and I first met him when he was 15 years old—and the kind of man he was, he preferred to disappear into the background.

Larry's personality was just the opposite of Jackie's. Doby was a better ballplayer than Robinson, had more power, and was faster, but he didn't have Jackie's leadership qualities. He was quiet, not very outgoing, maybe even aloof. And he played in the more conservative Midwest, in small-market Cleveland, not a media capital like New York.

I had heard a lot about Doby when he was just in high school. He grew up in Paterson, New Jersey, not far from where I grew up in Orange. He was six years younger than me, but Larry and my youngest brother, Calvin, were good friends. They competed against each other. I became aware of Doby because I had been all-state in four sports, and then Larry came along and he was the next one in New Jersey to be all-state in four sports. (He was also the last one to do that until Willie Wilson came along about 40 years later.)

In 1943, when he was just 18, Larry signed with the Newark Eagles and became my teammate and my double-play partner. When Willie Wells left the Eagles, I was moved from center field to play shortstop, and Doby was my second baseman. Let me tell you, he could play second base. When he got to Cleveland, the Indians had Joe Gordon playing second base, so they moved Doby to center field, a position he had never played. The next year, Doby made the All-Star team as a center fielder and the Indians won the World Series with him in center, so he played center field for the Indians for the next seven years. That's how good Larry Doby was.

He led the American League in home runs twice, hit over .300 twice, drove in more than 100 runs five times, and made the All-Star team seven times.

When his major league playing career was over, Larry played one year in Japan and then coached for the Expos, Indians, and White Sox. Midway through the 1978 season, Doby replaced Bob Lemon as manager of the Chicago

White Sox for the final 87 games. Three years earlier, Frank Robinson had become the first black manager in baseball history when he was hired to manage the Cleveland Indians. So, once again, Doby was second.

Always a bridesmaid, never a bride!

Who was Detroit's greatest outfielder?

If you say Ty Cobb, you'll get no argument from me, or from anybody else.

Who was the next-best Detroit outfielder?

Harry Heilmann? Al Kaline? How about Norman "Turkey" Stearnes? Who?

Turkey Stearnes played for the Detroit Stars for 11 years and won three Negro National League batting titles, more than any other player except

Turkey Stearnes won three Negro National League batting titles and six home-run titles playing for his hometown Detroit Stars.

Willard Brown. He also won six home-run championships, and research shows that he hit more than 140 home runs in 585 games in his career.

I saw Turkey play one time in Newark when I was 12 or 13 years old. He was a left-handed hitter who batted leadoff, and he hit with his foot in the bucket, like Al Simmons from the right side. And he could run. First time up, he hit the first pitch over the center-field fence, and by the time the ball left the park, Turkey was at second base.

I got to meet Stearnes at a reunion of Negro Leagues players in 1974 or 1975 in Kentucky. He had come from Detroit, where to make ends meet during the off-season he had worked for years in automobile plants. He had cancer when I met him, and he died just two or three years later.

He was a great player, but not many people know much about him, which is true of so many Negro Leagues players from the 1920s and 1930s. For years his name came up for the Hall of Fame, but he wasn't elected. Cool Papa Bell said, "If there's any question about whether Turkey Stearnes should be in the Hall of Fame, take me out and put him in."

Turkey was finally inducted in 2000, 21 years after his death.

Career Summaries

Center Fielder	Years	Teams
Willie Mays *Batted over .300 in two of his three seasons with Black Barons*	1948–50	Birmingham Black Barons
Oscar Charleston *Hit three home runs in 1935 Negro Leagues World Series victory for Crawfords*	1915–44	Indianapolis ABCs, Lincoln Stars, Chicago American Giants, St. Louis Giants, Harrisburg Giants, Hilldale Daisies, Homestead Grays, Pittsburgh Crawfords, Philadelphia Stars, Brooklyn Brown Dodgers, Indianapolis Clowns
Cool Papa Bell *Hit .407 (11–27) for Stars against Chicago in 1928 Negro National League playoff series*	1922–46	St. Louis Stars, Pittsburgh Crawfords, Detroit Wolves, Kansas City Monarchs, Chicago American Giants, Homestead Grays
Larry Doby *Scored 41 runs in 43 games in 1946*	1942–47	Newark Eagles
Turkey Stearnes *Led Negro National League in both batting average and home runs in 1931*	1920–40	Nashville Giants, Montgomery Grey Sox, Detroit Stars, Lincoln Giants, Chicago American Giants, Philadelphia Stars, Kansas City Monarchs

EIGHT

Right Fielder

Henry Aaron played only one year in the Negro Leagues, with the Indianapolis Clowns in 1952. He was only 18 years old at the time. I didn't see Aaron with Indianapolis because I was with the New York Giants by then, but I saw plenty of him in the major leagues. Henry was the last player from the Negro Leagues to reach the majors.

The first time I saw Henry was in 1954 when he came up with the Milwaukee Braves, and I was immediately impressed with his ability, not only as a hitter, but in all facets of the game. He could run, he could steal bases, he had a great arm, and he could field. He had the quickest wrists of any hitter I have ever seen.

When he was young, he used to hit cross-handed. One day I asked him, "How did you hit a curveball batting that way?"

"I don't know," he said, "but I hit it."

Henry could do everything, but for all his greatness, there always seemed to be something missing in Aaron's game that prevented him from getting the recognition he deserved, the same recognition Willie Mays got. Henry

1. HENRY AARON

2. CRISTÓBAL TORRIENTE

3. BILL WRIGHT

4. SAM JETHROE

5. JIMMIE CRUTCHFIELD

Henry Aaron played only one season in the Negro Leagues, but we all know what he did when he went to the majors after a one-year stint with the Indianapolis Clowns at age 18. He'll go down as one of *the* greatest players of all time, and some will argue the greatest.

had no flair. He just went out there and did it. Mays had charisma. Henry didn't have it. He wasn't even a big drawing card. Mays was a drawing card.

Aaron showed his class, his poise, and his dignity, suffering in silence as he chased, and surpassed, baseball's most cherished record, Babe Ruth's mark of 714 career home runs. He received hundreds of death threats and racial slurs but never complained and never caved in to the pressure.

Who would ever have thought that this young fellow from Mobile, Alabama, could have beaten Babe Ruth? You just never thought of him in that light, but he hung in there and he didn't get injured very much. He became the all-time home-run king, and it was my privilege to be in Atlanta, representing Commissioner Bowie Kuhn, when Henry hit the 715th home run of his career off Al Downing and passed Ruth's record.

Despite breaking the all-time home-run record, Aaron never hit 50 home runs in a season. His best was 47 in 1971. He also benefited when the Braves moved from Milwaukee to Atlanta, where all he had to do was get the ball in the air to hit it out. If the Braves had stayed in Milwaukee, I'm not sure he would have broken the home-run record.

But take nothing away from Aaron. He was consistent and he had longevity, and he rates as one of the greatest players of all time.

Aaron played in an era that many people say produced the game's greatest players, like Henry and Mays, Frank Robinson, Roberto Clemente, Bob Gibson, and Ferguson Jenkins.

As great as those guys were, there were others playing in the Negro Leagues before them who were just as great and who would have made an impact in the big leagues. That's what I mean when I say baseball missed out on seeing some great players from the Negro Leagues who never got the chance to show what they could do in the major leagues.

We were playing an All-Star Game in Mexico, and I made one of the greatest throws you've ever seen. Best throw I ever made, from center field to home plate on a line. I couldn't throw a ball better than that.

I was living with another player named Quincy Trouppe, a catcher who played in six games for the Cleveland Indians in 1952, and after the game we went back to our apartment and I was feeling pretty good about myself. I asked Quincy, "Did you ever see a better throw than that?"

"Yeah," he said. "I saw one other man make a throw that was a little better than yours."

"Who was that?" I asked.

"**Cristóbal Torriente**," he said.

"Well, get your things and get the hell out of here," I said.

I never saw Torriente play, but those who did tell me he was something special, a Cuban who played from 1914 to 1932 with several teams, including the Cuban Stars, the Chicago American Giants, and the Kansas City Monarchs. They say he could do it all, that he was a home-run hitter and had a great arm and great personality. He was a left-handed power hitter and a sure-handed fielder with excellent speed. He's revered in Cuba.

They used to call him a one-man ballclub because he could play any position and play it well. He started his career as a center fielder with the Chicago American Giants, but as he got older he moved around to other positions. He played all three outfield positions and also played a lot of infield, second base, and third, and they say he handled both positions expertly, not handicapped by being a left-handed thrower.

Cristóbal Torriente was an all-around talent who is revered in his homeland of Cuba, much in the way Babe Ruth is revered in the United States. As with Ruth, some of the legends of Torriente's feats border on the mythical.

He also pitched and had a career record of 15–5. He could have been a star pitcher in the Negro Leagues, but his bat was too potent to waste on the mound. Because of the similarities between them, Torriente was called "the Babe Ruth of Cuba."

I could put Cristóbal at any position on my team and not go wrong, but it seems logical to me to put "the Babe Ruth of Cuba" in right field.

They used to call Torriente a one-man ballclub because he could play any position and play it well.

There are so many stories that have been passed down through the years about Torriente's exploits that it's hard to know which are real and which are fantasy. One story is that in Kansas City he hit a line drive so hard that it cracked a clock above the center-field fence and the hands of the clock kept going around and around.

Another story, which has been documented, is that in 1920 the New York Giants went to Cuba to play a series of exhibition games and brought Babe Ruth with them. In one game, Torriente hit home runs in his first two at-bats. When he came up a third time with runners on base, Ruth jogged in from right field and demanded he pitch to Torriente.

Torriente proceeded to drill a bases-clearing double off Ruth, who finished off the inning by striking out the next three hitters before returning to the outfield. Later in the game, with Ruth back in right field, Torriente hit a third home run.

Another story that seems to have some basis in truth is that early in the 1920s the New York Giants had a scout following the Monarchs and were close to signing Torriente. Although he was a light-skinned Cuban, Torriente had kinky hair, and the Giants figured that despite his pigmentation, Torriente wouldn't be able to pass, so sadly, they never attempted to sign him.

Think of Dave Parker, the slugging outfielder for the Pittsburgh Pirates, and you have a mental picture of "Wild" **Bill Wright**. Like Parker, Wright was big and strong, a terrific hitter, and an excellent fielder with a great arm, and he could fly. He was also the nicest guy in the world. If anybody belongs in the Hall of Fame, it's Bill Wright.

Wright broke in with the Nashville Elite Giants in 1932 and batted .300 as a rookie. By 1938 the Giants had moved to Baltimore after stops in Columbus, Ohio, and Washington, D.C., and Wright was perhaps the most feared hitter in the Negro National League, batting .410. The following year, he led the league with an incredible .488 batting average. In 1943 he won another

Bill Wright, who became a legend in Mexico after playing in the Negro Leagues, batted an incredible .488 to take the crown in the Negro National League in 1939.

batting title and the Triple Crown. He won the home-run title by one over Roy Campanella and tied Ray Dandridge for the league lead in RBIs. And he also missed by one the league's stolen-base title.

Wright twice left Baltimore to play in Mexico, where he became a fan favorite. He went back to Baltimore in 1945, but after the season, he returned to Mexico for good. Bill was one of four or five guys from the Negro Leagues who went to Mexico, because there, for the first time in their lives, they felt free. They found that in Mexico they didn't have to deal with the discrimination they encountered in the United States.

Wright spent the last 10 years of his career playing in Mexico and became a national hero. Although he did not make the Hall of Fame in this country, he was elected to the Mexican Baseball Hall of Fame in 1972.

Bill spent the remainder of his days in Mexico except for a trip back to Chicago in 1991 to attend a reunion of Negro Leagues players. He died in Mexico six years later.

People who followed the Negro Leagues say that Cool Papa Bell was the fastest runner they have ever seen. I have no reason to doubt that Bell was fast. I never saw him play, but I played with **Sam Jethroe** for two years, and if Cool Papa could run faster than Jethroe, I sure would love to have seen him.

Sam could flat-out fly. They called him "the Jet."

A switch-hitter and the ideal leadoff batter, he was the premier base stealer of his time in the Negro Leagues and the only player ever to hit a ball over the 472-foot fence in Toledo's Swayne Field and into the coal piles of the Red Man Tobacco factory. Jethroe began his career with the Cincinnati (later Cleveland) Buckeyes in 1942 and actually got a major league try-out in 1945. Sportswriter Wendell Smith of *The Pittsburgh Courier,* who had been a longtime advocate for breaking the color line in the major leagues, arranged for Sam, Jackie Robinson, and Marvin Williams to get a tryout with the Boston Red Sox.

All three performed well enough to impress Red Sox manager Joe Cronin and coach Hugh Duffy, who both said Robinson, Jethroe, and Williams were good enough to play in the majors. Robinson said that at the tryout Jethroe "looked like a gazelle in the outfield."

A switch-hitter and the ideal leadoff batter, Sam Jethroe was the premier base stealer of his time in the Negro Leagues and the only player ever to hit a ball over the 472-foot fence in Toledo's Swayne Field and into the coal piles of the Red Man Tobacco factory.

Following his Negro Leagues career, Sam Jethroe went on to win the Rookie of the Year Award with the Boston Braves.

The tryout turned out to be a sham. The Red Sox obviously had no intention of signing them, and, in fact, Boston was the last major league team to integrate.

Robinson, Jethroe, and Williams were asked to fill out application blanks and were told they would hear from the Red Sox. They never did.

Three years later, Jethroe was still playing with the Cleveland Buckeyes when he was signed by Boston—the Braves, not the Red Sox—and sent to the International League, where he stole 89 bases. The next year, he became the first black player on the Braves. Sam got his chance, but like a lot of Negro Leagues players of that time, his chance came when his best years were behind him.

Still, Jethroe batted .273 for the Braves, hit 18 home runs, scored 100 runs, led the major league in stolen bases with 35, and was named 1950 National League Rookie of the Year. The books listed Jethroe as being 28 years old, but the common belief was that he was at least four or five years older than that, making him the oldest player ever to win the Rookie of the Year award.

Jethroe's 1951 numbers were almost identical to his rookie numbers—a .280 average instead of .273, 101 runs scored instead of 100, 65 RBIs instead of 58, and the same number of home runs (18) and stolen bases (35), again leading the majors.

In 1952 Jethroe's numbers began to slide dramatically. They said he suffered from poor vision, but other rumors that he was closer to 40 than the 30 years that the books listed persisted as well.

One look at 5'7" **Jimmie Crutchfield** would tell you the kind of ballplayer he was. As a hitter, he played the little man's game. He just slapped the ball around. He never hit a home run, although he might hit a double once in a while.

He could run, and he was a great fielder. When he played with the Pittsburgh Crawfords, he was one-third of what many say was the greatest Negro Leagues outfield ever—Crutchfield, Cool Papa Bell, and Ted Strong. All

The diminutive Jimmie Crutchfield was, in the words of Cool Papa Bell, "the best team player in baseball." *Photo courtesy of the Rucker Archive.*

three could run and catch the ball. Nothing ever dropped in that outfield. Satchel Paige said, "A rain drop wouldn't fall in that outfield."

Jimmie was very popular with fans. He had this engaging, outgoing, affable personality, and he liked to interact with the fans, which made him a big favorite.

Jimmie was my teammate for a while with the Newark Eagles, and I remember one game we were winning by one run with two outs in the bottom of the ninth and a couple of men on base. A ball was hit to center field, and Jimmie, who liked to put on a show for the crowd, caught it behind his back.

After the game, Effa Manley said to Crutchfield, "You scared me to death. If you do that again, it will cost you $500."

"Mrs. Manley," Jimmie replied, "you've seen the last of my behind-the-back catches."

Cool Papa Bell said that Crutchfield was "the best team player in baseball. If he [had] never played in a game he would still have been an important part of any baseball team. He cheered you up when things weren't going too good, whether you had troubles on or off the field. You always knew you could count on Jimmie to be on the bright side of things."

Career Summaries

Right Fielder	Years	Teams
Henry Aaron *Led Puerto Rican Winter League with nine home runs in 1954*	1952	Indianapolis Clowns
Cristóbal Torriente *Had the highest batting average (.350) in Cuban Winter League history*	1913–32	New York Cubans, All-Nations, Chicago American Giants, Detroit Stars, Kansas City Monarchs, Cleveland Cubs
Bill Wright *Played in nine East-West All-Star Games, batting .323*	1932–35	Nashville Elite Giants, Columbus Elite Giants, Washington Elite Giants, Baltimore Elite Giants, Philadelphia Stars
Sam Jethroe *Stole league-leading 52 bases in 70 games in 1947*	1942–48	Cincinnati Buckeyes, Cleveland Buckeyes
Jimmie Crutchfield *Four time All-Star between 1935 and 1941*	1930–45	Birmingham Black Barons, Indianapolis ABCs, Pittsburgh Crawfords, Newark Eagles, Toledo Crawfords, Chicago American Giants, Cleveland Buckeyes

NINE

Right-Handed Pitcher

Smokey" Joe Williams** stood head and shoulders above all Negro Leagues pitchers, literally and figuratively. And he was a giant in more ways than one. He played for, among others, the Leland Giants, Chicago Giants, Lincoln Giants, Chicago American Giants, Bacharach Giants, and Brooklyn Royal Giants, and he was a giant of a man at 6'5", 200 pounds, which was gigantic in his day (he played from 1910 to 1932).

Williams is unanimously regarded as the greatest Negro Leagues pitcher ever, and it's little wonder when you look at some of the things he accomplished. Records from his playing days are sketchy at best, but extensive research revealed the following about Williams:

1. "Smokey" Joe Williams

2. Satchel Paige

3. Leon Day

4. "Bullet" Joe Rogan

5. Martin Dihigo

- In the 1914 season, he won 41 games and lost only three.
- On August 2, 1930, pitching for the Homestead Grays, he struck out 27 batters, allowed one hit, and beat the Kansas City Monarchs, 1–0, in 12 innings. Chet Brewer pitched for the Monarchs, and he allowed

four hits and struck out 19, including 10 in a row starting in the seventh inning. So there were 46 strikeouts in that game. They say the lights were bad, but I don't care if you're playing in the dark, or playing stickball in the street, when you strike out 27 batters in a game, you've done something special. Smokey Joe was 44 years old at the time.

• He had a 20–7 record in exhibition games against major leaguers and defeated five Hall of Fame pitchers in head-to-head competition: Grover Cleveland Alexander, Chief Bender, Waite Hoyt, Rube Marquard, and Walter Johnson, with whom he drew comparisons because of his blazing fastball.

"Smokey" Joe Williams, who Ty Cobb himself said would be a 30-game winner in the majors, is widely considered the best pitcher in Negro Leagues history.

Williams threw so hard that opponents and teammates gave him the nick-names "Cyclone" and "Strikeout." After he struck out 20 New York Giants in an exhibition game, Giants outfielder Ross Youngs patted Joe on the rear end and said, "Nice job, Smokey," and that nickname stuck.

The great hitter Ty Cobb once said that Williams would have been "a sure 30-game winner" if he had been allowed to pitch in the major leagues.

Even Satchel Paige, a pretty good pitcher himself, said that Smokey Joe was the greatest pitcher he ever saw.

Frank Leland, the owner of the Leland Giants, once said about Williams, "If you have ever witnessed the speed of a pebble in a storm you have not seen the equal of the speed possessed by this wonderful Texan. You have to see him but once to exclaim, 'That's aplenty.'"

I never saw Williams pitch, but I did get to meet him in 1940 after he had retired from baseball and was tending bar in Harlem.

Williams had no children and has no known relatives alive, so very little is known about Smokey Joe except that he was born on or about April 6, 1886, in Seguin, Texas, a small town about 50 miles east of San Antonio. A group from his hometown is trying to put together a memorial to this great pitcher who finally got his due when he was elected to the Hall of Fame in 1999.

He was not the best player in the Negro Leagues, and by most estimates, he wasn't even the best pitcher. But there is no denying that Leroy "Satchel" Paige was the most popular, most famous, most intriguing, most charismatic, most colorful character ever to play in the Negro Leagues. Also, he was their greatest gate attraction.

Folks who are not even baseball fans and others who know little or noth-ing about Negro Leagues baseball know the name **Satchel Paige**. He was a folk hero and a legendary figure in this country for more than half a century.

Satchel was one of a kind, marching to the beat of his own drum. In some ways he *was* Negro Leagues baseball. In other ways, he was bigger than the game itself.

When most Negro Leagues games would draw only a few hundred fans, Satch filled ballparks whenever and wherever he pitched.

While the average salary for even the best Negro Leagues players was $200 per month, between his Negro Leagues pay and the money he made on barn-storming tours, Satch was pulling down anywhere from $30,000 to $40,000 per year. There even is a report that in one year in the 1940s, when he and

The incomparable Satchel Paige, in many respects, was the public face of the Negro Leagues and remains so to this day.

Bob Feller joined forces on a barnstorming tour, Satch pocketed a whopping $100,000.

Satch had his own airplane that he flew on his barnstorming trips, which he once admitted gave him more satisfaction (and more money) than playing in the Negro Leagues.

"I liked playing against Negro Leagues teams," he said, "but I loved barnstorming. It gave us a chance to play everybody and go everywhere and let millions of people see what we could do. I just loved it. I'd have played every day of the year if I could."

Most accounts fix Paige's birth date as July 7, 1906, and his birthplace as Mobile, Alabama, but there are those who insist there is evidence that he was actually born seven years earlier. As a boy he ran with a rough crowd, frequently played hooky from school, got into fights, was often in trouble with the police, and earned pocket money by toting bags at the local railroad station. He creatively rigged a pole with ropes to make a sling that enabled him to carry three or four bags at a time, thereby increasing his income. One redcap, noticing the device, said, "You look like a walking satchel tree," and that's how he got his nickname, not, as is widely believed, from his size-12 feet.

Paige's troubles as a juvenile landed him in reform school, and it was there that he discovered his gift for pitching. Upon release from reform school, he began playing for semipro teams in and around Mobile. Soon his reputation as a pitcher grew, and he became known throughout the South. In 1928 he was sold to the Birmingham Black Barons of the Negro National League and embarked on a career that would become legendary.

Starting out, he was a tall, gangly teenager, 6'3½" and 140 pounds. As he got older, he added about 40 pounds, but he never lost his rail-thin, gangly look. At first he threw nothing but fastballs, and he could really bring it, straight overhand and with unerring control. Nobody threw harder than Satch. Later he dropped down and threw sidearm, submarine style, all sorts of deliveries. He liked to give his various pitches a name.

He called his fastball his "bee ball," "hump ball," "trouble ball," or "Long Tom." There was also his "Bat Dodger" and his famous "Hesitation Pitch," which he delivered after pausing briefly as his front (left) foot hit the ground.

*I*t was a meaningless, inconsequential three-game September series between the American League's two bottom-feeders, the ninth-place Boston Red Sox and the 10th-place Kansas City Athletics, in 1965. Well, it was meaningless and inconsequential except for one thing: in the middle game, on Saturday night, September 25, Satchel Paige—the ageless, legendary, and charismatic star of the Negro Leagues—was the starting pitcher for the Athletics.

Old Satch, by best estimates 59 years old at the time (but quite possibly seven years older than that), would thereby become the oldest man to appear in a major league game.

It was the brainchild of Kansas City's maverick new owner, Charles O. Finley, who clearly was looking for any way to bring people into his ballpark. His ragtag team, two years away from moving to Oakland and six years away from becoming an American League power, would finish 10th in the American League with a record of 59–103 and 10th in attendance with 528,344.

On the surface, the gimmick seemed to go over like a lead balloon, as only 9,289 paid their way into Kansas City's Municipal Stadium to see the great Satchel pitch. However, contrasted against Friday night's attendance of 2,304 and Sunday afternoon's attendance of 2,874, Finley could boast that his spectacle produced some 7,000 additional paid admissions.

Matched up against Paige was a 29-year-old native of Medford, Massachusetts (a suburb of Boston), named Bill Monbouquette, who was in his final season with the Red Sox. He had pitched a no-hitter three years earlier and won 20 games the year after that. In his sometimes-spectacular career, he won 114 games and played with Hall of Famers Ted Williams and Carl Yastrzemski in Boston; Al Kaline in Detroit; Whitey Ford and Mickey Mantle in New York; and Willie Mays, Willie McCovey, Juan Marichal, and Gaylord Perry in San Francisco, but he remembers the game against Paige as the highlight of a wonderful career.

"Leading up to all this, the A's got a rocking chair and put it in the bullpen," said Monbouquette. "So for a few nights, Satchel just went down to the bullpen and sat there rocking away. Tony Conigliaro kept saying he couldn't wait to hit against him. 'I'll take that old guy out of the park,' Tony C. said."

In the top of the first, Paige retired Jim Gosger on a pop fly to first baseman Santiago Rosario. Dalton Jones smashed one through Rosario for an error, and when the ball ricocheted off the right-field stands, Jones was thrown out trying to go to third. Yastrzemski then lined a double, and Conigliaro had a chance to make good on his boast. He flied to left fielder Tommie Reynolds.

In the second inning, Lee Thomas popped to third baseman Wayne Causey, Felix Mantilla popped to shortstop Bert Campaneris, and Ed Bressoud flied to right fielder Mike Hershberger.

In the third inning, Mike Ryan popped to Campaneris, Monbouquette struck out, and Gosger grounded to Campaneris.

Paige had pitched three innings, allowed one hit, walked none, and struck out one.

"He was throwing pretty good," Monbouquette said. "They weren't using radar guns in those days, but I'd guess he was getting it up there about 86, 88 miles an hour. I don't know how old he was, but I figure he had to be in his sixties, and he had better swings off me than I did off him."

As Paige's only strikeout victim that night in Kansas City, Monbouquette—who pitched a complete-game seven-hitter in the 5–2 Red Sox win, his 10th win of the season—was the last batter Satch struck out in the major leagues.

"I had seen him pitch against the Red Sox when I was a kid and he was with Cleveland," Monbouquette remembered. "He threw real hard then, and with great control, and he was almost 50. My only regret is that when I pitched against him in Kansas City, I never got the chance to meet him and talk to him. I wish now that I had."

Double Duty Radcliffe, a pretty fair country pitcher himself, said about Paige: "What made him great was his fastball. It was overpowering. I mean overpowering. But it wasn't just his speed. He had fantastic location. He could throw 105 miles per hour and hit a mosquito flying over the outside corner of the plate."

Oh, old Satch could be a pain in the butt. He liked to party, and there were times he'd be partying when he should have been at the ballpark. If he saw a pretty girl, he might go wherever she was going rather than to the ballpark.

He often failed to show up for games, and he didn't believe in the sanctity of the contract. He thought nothing of running out on his contract and jumping from one team to another.

Satch bounced from team to team (he played for, among others, the Chattanooga Black Lookouts, Birmingham Black Barons, Cleveland Cubs, Pittsburgh Crawfords, Kansas City Monarchs, New York Black Yankees, and Philadelphia Stars), often leaving one team and signing with another that offered him more money. And he was just as often sent packing by an owner who, despite Satch's greatness on the field and at the box office, tired of his antics and couldn't wait to get rid of him. When Gus Greenlee, owner of the Crawfords, offered Paige a salary of $450 per month, Satch told Greenlee, "I wouldn't throw ice cubes for that kind of money."

When Paige and Feller were partners on their barnstorming tour, Feller hired Dizzy Dismukes, who had been the manager of the Monarchs, to make sure Satchel got to the plane and ballpark on time. Paige and Feller would pitch against each other frequently on their tour, and they hooked up in some memorable, classic battles. One night they were scheduled to face each other in Los Angeles. Feller said, "Satch, I'm giving up nothing tonight." And Satch said, "Me either, Bob." So neither one of them gave up a run, and the game was called a tie after 10 innings.

When Paige was scheduled to pitch, an additional 5,000 to 10,000 people would show up just to see him, and Satch's deal usually called for him to get a percentage of the gate. It got to the point where he was pitching every night, at least a couple of innings, just to draw a crowd and fatten his bank account.

As irresponsible as Satch was, there never was any resentment of him by the other players, because when he got on the mound, he was all business. He was so magnificent that he made you forget about his foibles. He had such charisma and was such a showman and a crowd-pleaser. I never heard him say he was going to do something in a game and then not do it. Sure, he liked to showboat, but he always delivered.

He would say he was going to strike out the first six men or the first nine men in a game, and he'd do it. Or he would call his outfielders in and pitch without any outfielders, and nobody would hit a ball out of the infield.

I first saw Satchel in Puerto Rico in 1941. He struck me out three times, and after the game he came and talked to me. He didn't call me "Monte"; he called me "young-un." Satch never called anybody by their name; he always had special names for them, probably because he could never remember names.

He said, "You know, young-un, you'll never hit me the way you hold your bat. You've got your bat way up there. By the time you bring it down, I'm by your inside and gone."

I said, "What do you suggest?"

"You've got to drop your bat," he said. "Get that bat down a little bit if you expect to hit me."

Later on that year, I faced him in Yankee Stadium in the Negro Leagues All-Star Game, and I hit a double off of him. He called timeout and came out to second base and said, "See? I told you that you were going to be a success, you were going to be a better hitter."

The last time I hit against Satch was in a spring training game in Phoenix. The count went to 3–2, and I figured he had to throw me a fastball. I sat on a fastball, but Satch dropped this beautiful curveball on me, right over the heart of the plate. It fooled me so much, I couldn't pull the trigger and I just watched it go by, and then I heard the umpire say, "Ball four."

Obviously, the pitch surprised the umpire just like it surprised me. He was looking for a fastball, too.

Satch couldn't believe it, and there he came toward home plate. He stopped halfway between the pitcher's mound and home and said to the umpire, "What's the matter with it? Was it too good?"

Paige had a rubber arm. He pitched for more than 30 years, winter and summer. Often he would pitch every other day, sometimes every day.

There are no official records, but Paige's own estimate is that he pitched in more than 2,500 games (153 in one year), won about 2,000, threw about 100 no-hitters, and pitched for 250 teams. Even allowing for some exaggeration, and even if he wasn't always pitching against topflight competition, the numbers are staggering.

In 1948 Bill Veeck signed him for the Cleveland Indians. At 42, Paige was the oldest rookie in major league history. Paige appeared in 21 games for the Indians, had a record of 6–1, made seven starts, completed three, and pitched two shutouts.

In his first three starts, he drew more than 201,000 fans, including a still-standing major league record attendance of 78,382 in Cleveland's Municipal Stadium on August 20, 1948, beating the Chicago White Sox, 1–0, on a complete-game three-hitter. He was the first African American to pitch in the American League and the first to pitch in a World Series, working

131

two-thirds of an inning in Game 5 of the Indians' six-game victory over the Boston Braves.

Satch was let go by the Indians after the 1949 season, but when Veeck took over as owner of the St. Louis Browns, he brought Paige back in 1951, and Satch stayed through the 1953 season. Three years later, Paige and Veeck teamed up again when the flamboyant Veeck ran the Miami team in the International League.

Paige was to have one more shot at major league hitters. In 1965, at the age of 59, give or take a few years, the Kansas City Athletics signed him as a gate attraction and public-relations gimmick and started him in one game, against the Boston Red Sox of Carl Yastrzemski and Tony Conigliaro on September 25. Satch pitched three innings; allowed no runs, one hit, and no walks; and struck out one.

In 1961 Paige published his autobiography in which he revealed his prescription for eternal youth, as follows:

Avoid fried meats, which angry up the blood.

If your stomach disputes you, lie down and pacify it with cool thoughts.

Keep the juices flowing by jangling gently as you move.

Go very light on the vices, such as carrying on in society—the society rumble ain't restful.

Avoid running at all times.

And don't look back. Something might be gaining on you.

His autobiography was titled *Maybe I'll Pitch Forever*.
Satch almost did.

A lot of people don't know what a great pitcher **Leon Day** was. He was as good as or better than Bob Gibson. He was a better fielder than Gibson and a better hitter. When he pitched against Satchel Paige, Satchel didn't have an edge. If you think Don Newcombe could pitch, you should have seen Leon Day. One of the most complete athletes I've ever seen.

Leon started out as a second baseman with the Baltimore Red Sox. He was a terrific ballplayer, quick as a cat and could run like a deer, and he didn't have an enemy in the world. Everybody loved Leon. He could play the infield or the outfield and play them well, but he became a star as a pitcher.

*T*he dominant pitcher of his time—the author of three no-hitters, 12 one-hitters, 45 shutouts, six 20-win seasons, 266 career victories, and 2,581 strikeouts despite losing four playing years to military service during World War II—Bob Feller was secure enough in his ability and his status to put it all on the line in head-to-head competition with his counterpart from the Negro Leagues, the incomparable Satchel Paige.

Of course, there was money to be made, big money in barnstorming tours in the 1940s. But if money was Feller's primary motivation, there also was a risk, and a challenge, attached. His ego, his pride, and his reputation were all at stake competing against Paige, a man Feller has called "one of the legends of baseball and one of the top 10 pitchers in the history of our sport."

They had pitched against each other in barnstorming games prior to World War II—hired hands, paid a salary by various promoters—but it was the spectacle of Paige opposing Feller on the mound that brought fans flocking to those games in small towns across the country. And that gave Feller an idea.

After he was discharged from the navy, Feller decided to strike out on his own. He formed two teams, the Bob Feller All-Stars, consisting of top-notch major leaguers such as Stan Musial, Mickey Vernon, Phil Rizzuto, Bob Lemon, Charlie Keller, Eddie Lopat, and Jim Hegan, and the Satchel Paige All-Stars, made up of the best players from the Negro Leagues.

"I paid Satch and his players and all of mine, plus my airplane crews, a trainer, a physician, a secretary, a lawyer, a publicity man, and an advance man," Feller writes in his autobiography, *Now Pitching: Bob Feller*, written with Bill Gilbert and published by Birch Lane Press in 1990. "We ran everything first class, staying in the best hotels, flying in those DC-3s when they were the best in the air, and I was paying first-class salaries ranging from $1,700 for the month to $7,000."

Years later, Paige would say that those barnstorming games helped get him elected to the Baseball Hall of Fame in 1971. For that, he could thank Bob Feller, who would later be his teammate when the Cleveland Indians signed Satch as a 42(?)-year-old rookie in 1948.

> Said Feller:
>
> *Those games gave him the showcase he needed to display his pitching ability. When Cooperstown was integrated, the case for Satchel Paige had been made in part by what baseball people saw in his outstanding performances against my barnstorming team of top major leaguers.*
>
> *No ad agency or writer could have created a character like Satchel Paige. Only the good Lord can be that creative.*
>
> *Satch and I were friends, teammates and business associates. We were together in one capacity or another for almost my whole pitching career. We were a successful partnership, always aboveboard with each other. We worked hard for each other in our mutual endeavors and at the end of our projects, we were still friends.*

Day threw exceptionally hard, especially for someone who was only 5'9" and 170 pounds. He also had an outstanding curveball and good control. If his team didn't get any runs for him, he'd go up and hit a home run and win his own game.

Although he never got to play in the major leagues, Leon left his mark in baseball. He's credited with being the first pitcher to use the no-windup delivery. He could get rid of the ball so fast. There was only one criticism made of him: he was too quiet. He never argued with umpires, never tooted his own horn. He didn't believe in mouthing off. He'd just go out there and do it.

Leon has something in common with Bob Feller, Carl Hubbell, and Roger Clemens.

Feller pitched the only Opening Day no-hitter in the major leagues, and in 1946, in his first game back from military service, pitching for the Newark Eagles, Day threw the only Opening Day no-hitter in Negro Leagues history.

Hubbell struck out five straight future Hall of Famers in the 1934 major league All-Star Game, and Day struck out the first seven batters in the 1942 Negro Leagues All-Star Game.

Later that season, Leon set a Negro Leagues record when he struck out 18 Baltimore Elite Giants, including Roy Campanella three times. Forty-four years later, pitching for the Boston Red Sox, Roger Clemens set the major league record when he struck out 20 Seattle Mariners.

Leon Day's .708 career winning percentage is higher than any other Hall of Fame pitcher's, black or white.

When he retired, Day had a winning percentage of .708, which is higher than any pitcher, black or white, in the Hall of Fame.

Day was elected to the Hall of Fame in 1995. Happily, he was still alive to see it. Unhappily, he got the worst break in the world. If he had lived even a few months after he was inducted in the Hall of Fame, he could have left his wife a lot of money. A promoter had lined up about $100,000 in endorsements for him, but Leon was in the hospital when he learned he was elected to the Hall of Fame, and he died only a few days after the announcement.

Name a pitcher who was a good enough hitter to bat cleanup for his team.

All right, I'll give you Babe Ruth, but who else?

There was one in the Negro Leagues. His name was **"Bullet" Joe Rogan**, and in 1922 he led the Negro National League in home runs with 16.

His nickname tells you about his pitching. His fastball was his out pitch, and he also included a curveball, forkball, palmball, and spitball in his repertoire.

George "Tank" Carr, a teammate of Rogan's with the Kansas City Monarchs, called him "the greatest pitcher that ever threw a ball. And don't think Rogan was named 'Bullet' for nothing. That guy had a ball that was almost too fast to catch. He could really burn them in there."

But his ability as a pitcher is only part of Rogan's story. On a powerful team like the Monarchs that had Buck Leonard and Josh Gibson, Rogan usually batted fourth, fifth, or sixth. He is regarded as the greatest fielding pitcher in Negro Leagues history. And in one doubleheader, he pitched and played four other positions.

"Bullet" Joe Rogan not only had a blazing fastball but is also regarded as the greatest hitting and fielding pitcher in Negro Leagues history.

Rogan spent almost 10 years playing on army teams and didn't join the Monarchs until he was 30 years old, and then he spent almost 20 years with them. Records show that he was born in 1889 and that his final season with Kansas City was 1938, making him 49 years old when he retired.

Bullet Joe truly was a man who did it all in baseball. In addition to his great playing career, he had two tours as manager of the Monarchs, from 1926 to 1929 and from 1931 to 1938. And when he finally took off the uniform, he umpired in the Negro Leagues for several years, too.

I could put **Martin** (pronounced Marteen) **Dihigo** on my list of the top five at any position on the field except catcher. He played them all.

Buck Leonard called the big Cuban "the greatest all-around player I've ever seen. I say he was the best player of all time, black or white. He could do it all."

Johnny Mize, who played with Dihigo in the Dominican Republic Winter League, said, "He was the only guy I ever saw who could play eight positions, manage, run like the wind, and bat fourth."

When they played together, Dihigo would bat third and Mize fourth, and people remember there were times when they would walk Dihigo to pitch to Mize. That's how good of a hitter Dihigo was. He was one of the greatest players I've ever seen, and hardly anybody knows him. I've mentioned his name to modern players, and they say, "Martin who?" and I say, "You wouldn't say that if you had seen him play."

When I worked in his office, Commissioner Bowie Kuhn once said to me, "Monte, tell me about Martin Dihigo."

I said, "He was just a shade under Satchel Paige as a pitcher, but he played every other position except catcher. He played first base, second base, and shortstop. He played anywhere. He had a rifle for an arm; he could hit. A big, tall, regal, confident kind of a person. He knew he was good."

And he had a sense of humor. He was a showman. Once when he was on third base he kept yelling at the pitcher, "You balked, you balked." He kept hollering as he began to walk toward home plate. Everything stopped, and everybody kept staring at Dihigo like he had gone mad. But Martin kept walking toward home plate, and the other team just watched him step on the plate and duck into the dugout. The crowd went wild, laughing and cheering, and there was Martin, sitting in the dugout with a smile on his face.

137

I played against Dihigo in Mexico. One night in Monterey the lights weren't very good, and he struck me out three times. I told him, "Martin, you SOB, wait until you come down to Mexico City, I'll get even with you."

He said, "You might get even with me then, but I got you three times tonight."

He was something. What a guy! He just exuded confidence, and he could play; he could really play. And yet most people in the United States don't know anything about him.

Martin Dihigo played every position except catcher and played them all well. Buck Leonard even called him the best all-around player in baseball.

He was a national hero in both his native Cuba and Mexico. He's the only player who was inducted into the baseball Hall of Fame in three countries: Cuba, Mexico, and the United States. In Cuba they called him "el Maestro" and "el Immortal."

In 1938 he was 18–2 with a 0.90 earned-run average in the Mexican League, and he also led the league in hitting with a .387 batting average. That year, he dueled Satchel Paige in a classic game that they still talk about in Mexico. Satch was suffering with a sore arm, so he had to abandon his usual style of pitching. Instead of throwing his high, hard one, he relied on his guile, a submarine delivery, and a lot of trick pitches.

For six innings, Paige and Dihigo were locked in a scoreless duel. In the seventh, Paige's control left him, and he loaded the bases with two walks and a single. Then he uncorked a wild pitch that brought in one run, giving Dihigo the lead.

Paige was removed for a pinch-hitter, and his team tied the score, but in the ninth inning, Dihigo won the game with a home run.

Dihigo won more than 200 games in the United States and Mexico, and he also won three Negro Leagues home-run titles and tied Josh Gibson for a fourth. Imagine that—a pitcher.

Special mention must be made of "Cannonball" Dick Redding. I don't know where to place him among the five greatest right-handed pitchers in Negro Leagues history because I never saw him pitch, but from what I have heard he belongs somewhere in the top five.

But who would I leave out to get Redding in the list? Not "Smokey" Joe Williams. Certainly not Satchel Paige. And I have to include Leon Day, "Bullet" Joe Rogan, and Martin Dihigo on my team.

I heard so much about Cannonball when I came to the Newark Eagles in 1938, Redding's last season. He was managing and still pitching at the age of 47 for the Brooklyn Royal Giants, but we didn't play them.

I heard that Redding once won 43 games for the Lincoln Giants, including 17 in a row, and that he pitched a no-hitter and struck out 17 in an Eastern League game.

So let's just say that my list of the "top five" right-handed pitchers in Negro Leagues history has six names on it. I'll let you choose in which order they should be rated. However you place them, you can't go wrong.

Although they don't measure up to the six I have mentioned, there were some other great right-handers in the Negro Leagues, such as Raymond Brown, Don Newcombe, Hilton Smith, Dan Bankhead, Connie Johnson, Joe Black, "Steel Arm" Johnny Taylor, "Toothpick" Sam Jones, Dave Barnhill, Terris McDuffie, and a great submarine pitcher for the Philadelphia Stars named Webster McDonald, who threw like Dan Quisenberry, Ted Abernathy, and Chad Bradford and was nasty for right-handed batters.

Career Summaries

Right-Handed Pitcher	Years	Teams
"Smokey" Joe Williams *Won 20 of 27 decisions against major leaguers in postseason barnstorming games*	1910–32	Leland Giants, Chicago Giants, Lincoln Giants, Chicago American Giants, Bacharach Giants, Brooklyn Royal Giants, Homestead Grays, Detroit Wolves
Satchel Paige *Winning pitcher in both 1934 and 1943 East-West All-Star Games*	1927–55	Birmingham Black Barons, Cleveland Cubs, Pittsburgh Crawfords, Kansas City Monarchs, Memphis Red Sox, Philadelphia Stars, Chicago American Giants, Chattanooga Black Lookouts, New York Black Yankees
Leon Day *Pitched in a record seven Negro Leagues All-Star Games*	1934–50	Brooklyn Eagles, Newark Eagles, Baltimore Elite Giants
"Bullet" Joe Rogan *Won two games in 1924 Negro Leagues World Series victory over Hilldale*	1920–38	Kansas City Monarchs

continued	Years	Teams
Martin Dihigo *Pitched no-hitters in Mexico, Puerto Rico, and Venezuela*	1923–45	Cuban Stars, New York Cubans, Homestead Grays, Hilldale Daisies, Baltimore Black Sox

TEN

Left-Handed Pitcher

Several years ago I was talking with Charlie Gehringer, the great Hall of Fame second baseman of the Detroit Tigers. I knew that Charlie had played against black players in barnstorming games, so I asked him if there were any black players that stood out in his mind.

Gehringer said, "There was a left-handed pitcher that was really good."

He was talking about **Willie Foster**.

Foster was the half brother of Rube Foster, the manager/owner/organizer/pioneer who is known as "the father of Negro Leagues baseball." Willie lived in Tarboro, North Carolina, and the Newark Eagles played a game down there one time. Foster was in his forties, and he had been forced to retire because of a sore arm, but he wanted to pitch batting practice, so we let him.

1. WILLIE FOSTER

2. SLIM JONES

3. ROY PARTLOW

4. JOHN DONALDSON

5. BARNEY BROWN

He got on the mound and had a funky pitching motion, and we couldn't hit him. As old as he was and with a bad arm, we still couldn't hit him.

Cum Posey, the owner of the Homestead Grays, called Foster "the greatest left-hander Negro baseball ever saw," and Bill Yancey remembers Foster for his guile in the latter part of his career. "That guy would give you 10 hits and shut you out," Yancey marveled. "He could really pitch."

Willie Foster was a master at changing speeds and was generally regarded as the greatest
Negro Leagues left-hander.

Many would argue that only Willie Foster ranks ahead of Andy Cooper as a left-handed pitcher in Negro Leagues baseball.

Cooper was a rarity for his time, in the Negro Leagues and the major leagues, a relief specialist. Like so many pitchers in his day, Cooper was used both as a starter and a reliever. But his specialty was relief. He holds the all-time Negro Leagues record for saves and was the closest thing in his day to what is now known as a closer.

Cooper, who was elected to the Hall of Fame in 2006, came out of Waco, Texas, and was the ace of the staff for both the Detroit Stars and Kansas City Monarchs in the 1920s. Using pinpoint control and a deceptive change of speeds, he won twice as many games as he lost for the Stars from 1920 to 1927 and was so coveted by the Monarchs that they traded five players to acquire him.

In 1929 Cooper helped pitch the Monarchs to the Negro National League pennant and later, as their manager, led the Monarchs to three more championships in the four years from 1937 to 1940.

In a 1937 playoff game against the Chicago American Giants, he took the ball himself at the age of 37 and pitched 17 innings.

Dave Malarcher, who managed Foster with the Chicago American Giants, said, "Willie Foster's greatness was that he had this terrific speed and a great, fast-breaking curveball and a dropball, and he was really a master of the change-of-pace. He could throw you a real fast one and then use the same motion and bring it up a little slower, and then a little slower yet. And then he'd use the same motion again, and zzzzz! He was really a great pitcher."

On the final day of the 1927 season, the American Giants met the Kansas City Monarchs in a doubleheader, needing to win both games to win the Negro National League pennant. Foster started both games and won them both, each time defeating "Bullet" Joe Rogan. Then he won two games and helped the American Giants win the Negro Leagues World Series.

After the 1929 season, Foster participated in a two-game series against a team of American League All-Stars. The major leaguers beat up Foster in the first game, but in the second game, Willie shut out the major leaguers over eight innings and struck out nine. After the game, Charlie Gehringer told him, "If I could paint you white, I could get $150,000 for you right now."

After he retired, Willie became head baseball coach of Alcorn State College in Mississippi, his alma mater.

The story of **Slim Jones** is one of the saddest I know. He came on the scene like a meteor burning brightly and just as quickly burned out at a very young age.

Slim was the Randy Johnson of his day: a tall, skinny left-hander, 6'6" and 185 pounds—which accounts for his nickname—with an overpowering fastball and just wild enough to be an intimidating presence on the mound. He was awesome, just like Randy.

When Slim was scheduled to pitch, the left-handed hitters suddenly came down with a touch of the flu or a strained muscle.

Satchel Paige was once asked to name the greatest left-handed pitcher he had ever seen, and he named Slim Jones. Pitching duels between Satch and Slim were the stuff of legend. In 1934 Jones had a record of 32–4, 23–3 in league competition. He squared off with Paige four times that season, Jones pitching for the Philadelphia Stars, Paige for the Pittsburgh Crawfords.

Neither pitched very well in their first meeting, Jones winning, 10–5, but they would hook up again after the season in a four-team charity benefit doubleheader at Yankee Stadium. More than 30,000 fans were at the stadium to see Jones pitch six perfect innings and take a 1–0 lead into the seventh, when Oscar Charleston broke up the perfect game. In the next inning, the Crawfords got two more hits and tied the game, 1–1.

In the ninth, the Stars put two runners on base, but Paige ended the threat by striking out the last two batters. At that point, the game was called because of darkness. A month later, the Crawfords and Stars met again at Yankee Stadium. Before the game, Bill "Bojangles" Robinson, the great tap dancer of his day and a big baseball fan, presented Paige and Jones with travel bags in honor of their effort in what Robinson called "the greatest game ever played." This time, Paige beat Jones, 3–1.

It's not hard to see how Slim Jones got his name, and with his fastball, size, and intimidating presence, he could be called the Randy Johnson of the Negro Leagues.

It was in this game that, legend has it, Slim threw the pitch that Josh Gibson supposedly hit clear out of Yankee Stadium.

By 1935 Jones's life began to spin out of control. He apparently had a drinking problem and a taste for the good life, and as fast as his money came in, that's how fast it went out. To make matters worse, he hurt his arm and was no longer the dominant, overpowering pitcher he had been.

In 1938 his arm was so bad that the Stars sent him home in the middle of the season to rest and recover. That winter, penniless and with a burned-out arm, Jones hung out at his favorite local bar, where he would get together with his buddies and teammates. Because he had no money, Slim's friends would pay for his drinks, but Jones was too proud to continue accepting charity. He tired of his friends treating him, so Slim pawned his overcoat.

Philadelphia had a tough winter that year, and Slim didn't have the money to get his coat back, so he went without a coat all winter. As a result, he caught pneumonia and died. He was only 25 years old.

When the Brooklyn Dodgers signed Jackie Robinson for their Montreal club in the International League in 1946, they also signed a veteran right-handed Negro Leagues pitcher named John Wright and sent him to Montreal.

But Wright did not pitch well in the International League, and in May, he was optioned out to a lower minor league team and replaced by another Negro Leagues veteran, left-hander **Roy Partlow**.

Roy Partlow played for several years in Puerto Rico, where he and Satchel Paige had some classic pitching duels.

Unfortunately, Roy struggled in the International League, and he, too, was optioned out before the season ended.

Partlow's troubles in Montreal were a surprise to me because I consider him to be one of the best left-handed pitchers I saw in my years in the Negro Leagues.

Roy was a hard thrower who came out of Cincinnati. He had a good curveball and was a good hitter. He started out with the Cincinnati Tigers and then moved to the Memphis Red Sox. From Memphis he went to the Homestead Grays, who had Josh Gibson and Buck Leonard to power the offense; a pitching staff that included Raymond Brown, who pitched like Red Ruffing; and Partlow, who was just like Lefty Gomez.

Partlow could play the outfield. He could run like crazy, and he was a great pitcher. He and Satchel Paige hooked up in some classic duels in Puerto Rico.

Unfortunately, when Partlow got his chance with the Dodgers, he was past his prime and never made it to the big leagues, another guy for whom the breaking of the color line came just a few years too late.

I never saw **John Donaldson**, who played long before I got to the Negro Leagues, but I have heard a lot about him from old-timers. They say he was something special, a left-hander with a nasty curveball.

There's a story that Donaldson once pitched three consecutive no-hitters, which is remarkable if true, but it has never been confirmed or documented. Johnny Vander Meer is the only major leaguer in more than a century to pitch two consecutive no-hitters, and that happened way back in 1938.

Pop Lloyd said Donaldson was the toughest left-hander he ever faced, and John McGraw said if Donaldson were white, his value would have been $50,000. And we're talking about the early 1920s, so what would he be worth on the open market today?

Donaldson started his career in 1912 with the Tennessee Rats, an entertainment and baseball-playing troupe that barnstormed through the Midwest. Later he played for the All-Nations Club, a team made up of players of several races, and it is for this team that he allegedly pitched three consecutive no-hitters. He also played for the Los Angeles White Sox, Kansas City Monarchs, Chicago Giants, Indianapolis ABCs, Brooklyn Royal Giants, and Detroit Stars.

John Donaldson, who was rumored to have once thrown three consecutive no-hitters, became the first full-time black scout for a major league team when the White Sox hired him after his playing career ended.

The following text appeared on a pre–World War I poster and gives some insight into the appeal of the All-Nation's team and the esteem in which Donaldson was held:

FEDERAL LEAGUE PARK
Sept. 24-5-6
ORIGINAL ABCs
vs.
WORLD'S ALL-NATIONS
Heralding the First Appearance of the World's All-Nations, composed of Hawaiians, Japanese, Cubans, Filipinos, Indians, Chinese, direct from their native countries.
The Great Donaldson will positively pitch one of these games
JOHN DONALDSON
The Greatest Colored Pitcher in the World. Donaldson pitched 65 games last season, winning 60 of them.

Donaldson was such a good hitter that near the end of his career, when he was no longer the pitcher he had been, the Monarchs played him in the outfield.

Elden Auker, who pitched against Babe Ruth in the American League, remembers playing against the Monarchs, with Donaldson in center field, in 1929.

"I was in college," Auker said, "and we played on an Arapaho Indian reservation in Kansas. I pitched against Satchel Paige, and I won, 2–1. Between innings, Donaldson would go out to his position in center field and squat like a catcher. The Monarchs catcher, a fellow named Tom Young, squatted behind home plate, and he and Donaldson played catch. They'd throw the ball back and forth to each other on a line from 300 feet away. If I hadn't seen it, I wouldn't have believed it."

When his playing days were over and the color line was broken, Donaldson was hired by the Chicago White Sox as the first full-time black scout for a major league team.

Barney Brown pitched like Eddie Lopat, a crafty left-hander. He pitched for the Cuban Stars, the Philadelphia Stars, and the New York Black Yankees, but then he went to play in Mexico and liked it so much that he stayed there until he went to Canada to play for Lloydminster in his last two years.

Curley Williams, who was my teammate with the Newark Eagles, said this about Brown: "Let me tell you, he was great. When we had him in Lloydminster, he'd throw two pitches that would hit the front of the plate that couldn't even get to the catcher. Then he'd come up there and strike the side out. And he was an old man, almost 50 years old. And just a little guy, too. Didn't weigh over 170 pounds. But he had so much stuff on the ball [that] he had guys swinging at the ball before it got to home plate. He was amazing."

Brown seemed to be ageless. He started his career with the Cuban Stars in 1931 and ended it with Lloydminster 25 years later, in 1956. He listed his birthday as October 23, 1912, but in 1985 when he passed away, his death certificate had his date of birth as October 23, 1907, so when he pitched in Lloydminster, he was 49 years old.

I must make special mention here of three other left-handed pitchers: Jimmy Hill, my teammate with the Newark Eagles; Andy Cooper, who pitched for the Detroit Stars, Chicago American Giants, St. Louis Stars, and Kansas City Monarchs in the 1920s and 1930s; and the great Cuban southpaw Manuel "Cocaina" Garcia.

Hill was an outstanding pitcher, a little guy, very slender like Ron Guidry, and he threw hard like Guidry.

Jimmy came from Lakeland, Florida, which was the spring training home of the Detroit Tigers, and he used to hang out at the ballpark and sometimes would pitch batting practice for the Tigers. Hank Greenberg took a liking to him and said he wished the Tigers were able to sign him, but that was years before the color line was broken.

Cooper was decades ahead of his time: a relief specialist, a rarity in his day. Saves weren't an official statistic in the 1920s and 1930s, but researchers went back over old box scores and determined that Cooper holds the all-time record for saves in the Negro Leagues. He received his due recognition posthumously when he was elected to the Hall of Fame in the class of 2006.

Garcia, who played for the Cuban Stars and the New York Cubans, is in the baseball Hall of Fame in Venezuela and the Dominican Republic, as well as in his native Cuba.

Career Summaries

Left-Handed Pitcher	Years	Teams
Willie Foster *Won five of seven Negro Leagues World Series decisions (two in 1926, two in 1927, and one in 1937)*	1923–37	Memphis Red Sox, Chicago American Giants, Homestead Grays, Kansas City Monarchs, Birmingham Black Barons, Pittsburgh Crawfords
Slim Jones *Struck out a league-leading 210 during the 1933 Puerto Rican Winter League season*	1933–38	Baltimore Black Sox, Philadelphia Stars
Roy Partlow *Posted a 1.49 ERA in 145 innings in the 1939 Puerto Rican Winter League*	1934–50	Cincinnati Tigers, Memphis Red Sox, Homestead Grays, Philadelphia Stars
John Donaldson *Pitched six no-hitters, including a perfect game*	1916–34	All-Nations, Chicago Giants, Indianapolis ABCs, Kansas City Monarchs, Detroit Stars, Brooklyn Royal Giants, Los Angeles White Sox

continued	Years	Teams
Barney Brown *Posted three consecutive 16-win seasons in Mexico from 1939 to 1941*	1931–49	Cuban Stars, Philadelphia Stars, New York Black Yankees

ELEVEN

Manager

Many years before the DiMaggios, the Boyers, and the Alous, the first families of baseball were the Delahantys and the Taylors.

Five Delahanty brothers—Ed, Frank, Jim, Joe, and Tom—played in the major leagues slightly before and after the turn of the 20th century. At about the same time, the Taylor brothers, C.I., Candy (Jim), Ben, and Johnny, were making their mark in the Negro Leagues.

The oldest of the Taylor brothers was named Charles, but everybody called him C.I.

C.I. Taylor was a mediocre player who earned his fame as a manager, organizer, pioneer, and executive. He is credited with being one of the founders of the Negro National League, its first vice president, and the one who discovered such stars as Oscar

1. C.I. TAYLOR

2. CANDY TAYLOR

3. BUCK O'NEIL

4. VIC HARRIS

5. DAVE MALARCHER

Charleston, Biz Mackey, Dave Malarcher, and Bingo DeMoss and is generally regarded as the finest manager in the history of Negro Leagues baseball. He is believed to be the first to hold clubhouse meetings before and after games to discuss strategy and the strengths and weaknesses of the opposition.

C.I. Taylor is considered to be one of the founders of the Negro Leagues and is credited with being the first to hold clubhouse meetings to discuss strategy before and after games.

156

Taylor was born in South Carolina in 1875. He studied at Atlanta's Clark College and served in the army during the Spanish-American War. After his discharge, Taylor embarked on his managerial career with teams in his native South Carolina and then ran the Birmingham Giants. Later he moved his team to Indianapolis, where, backed by the American Brewing Company, he guided the Indianapolis ABCs. By adding such stars as Charleston, Malarcher, DeMoss, and his brothers Ben and Jim, he turned the ABCs into a Negro Leagues powerhouse.

Taylor was a dignified and suave man. As a manager, he displayed uncommon patience and a knack for psychology, extracting from his players a sense of loyalty and decorum. With C.I. as their model, the Indianapolis ABCs conducted themselves in a gentlemanly manner, always well groomed and soft-spoken.

Known to be fair and honest with his players, C.I. was a man of integrity and high moral values. One incident speaks to his honesty and decency.

Late in his career, C.I. continued to play sporadically, almost to the age of 50, and would occasionally use himself as a pinch-hitter. In one game, he reportedly stole third base, sliding into the bag in a cloud of dust. The umpire called him safe, but C.I. picked himself up out of the dirt, brushed himself off, raised his hand, and announced to the crowd: "Ladies and gentleman, I am an honest man. The umpire's decision is incorrect. I therefore declare myself out."

Can you imagine Leo Durocher or Billy Martin doing something like that?

C.I. Taylor's younger brother Jim, known as "Candy," had an outstanding playing career as a third baseman. Some even say **Candy Taylor** was the best third baseman ever to come out of the Negro Leagues.

Playing third base and hitting third in the batting order, Candy helped his brother's Indianapolis ABCs win the 1916 Black World Championship by hitting .478 in a critical five-game series with the New York Lincoln Giants and then .360 in the World Series.

Later Candy followed in his brother's footsteps as a manager and earned a reputation as a master strategist. In demand, he bounced around to pilot more than a dozen teams in a 30-year managerial career and managed and won more games (a reported 775) than any other manager in Negro Leagues history. And he won three Negro National League pennants, one with the St. Louis Stars and two with the Homestead Grays.

Taylor was known for being a player's manager, taking a low-key approach with his men. He'd tell his players, "Do anything you want to do because I don't care if you hit standing on your head, as long as you hit."

Cool Papa Bell, who played for him, said Taylor "kept his players loose, and you loved to play for him."

Candy Taylor (right), shown here in the dugout with Cool Papa Bell, had a great playing career and then went on to manage for 30 more years, winning a reported 775 games, which would put him atop the all-time Negro Leagues list. *Photo courtesy of Bettmann/CORBIS.*

158

Taylor's one idiosyncrasy as a manager was that he was inordinately super-stitious. He steadfastly forbade his players to eat peanuts in the dugout, considering the practice bad luck. To press their skipper's buttons, the players would load their uniform pockets with peanut shells and when Taylor's back was turned, they'd strew the shells all over the dugout floor, thereby succeeding in drawing their manager's ire.

For all he contributed to baseball—as a player and a manager in the Negro Leagues, a coach and scout in the major leagues, and an all-around ambassador and historian of the game—it's a shame that **Buck O'Neil** is not in the Hall of Fame for his overall contribution to the sport. Buck, whose baseball career spanned seven decades, is one of the most revered and enduring figures, black or white, in the history of the game.

I can't think of anyone who has had a longer, or more varied, baseball career than Buck O'Neil had.

Buck began his career in 1937 with the Memphis Red Sox. He played for them briefly and then moved on to the Kansas City Monarchs, where he played and managed for 19 years, with two years out for service in the U.S. Navy.

As a player, he was the Monarchs' first baseman and a good one. He won the Negro Leagues batting title in 1940 with a .345 average and in 1946, the year after his return from the navy, with a .350 average. In 1942 he helped the Monarchs win the Negro American League title and then batted .353 in Kansas City's four-game sweep of the Homestead Grays to win the Negro Leagues World Series.

Buck Leonard called O'Neil "one of the best ball players I've ever seen. He would find the gap in the outfield and hit it there."

Jimmie Crutchfield said, "I respected Buck in the clutch. He was that type of hitter, a smart, intelligent ballplayer, a hustling ballplayer. You had to pitch very carefully to him."

In 1948 O'Neil was named manager of the Monarchs and led the team to four league championships. He's credited with helping to develop future major leaguers Ernie Banks, George Altman, Gene Baker, Francisco Herrera, Elston Howard, J.C. Hartman, Connie Johnson, Lou Johnson, Satchel Paige, Hank Thompson, and Bob Thurman.

In 1956 Buck left the Monarchs and took a job as a scout for the Chicago Cubs. Among his discoveries were Lou Brock and Joe Carter. Six years later, he made history by becoming the first African American coach in the major leagues. You might even say that he was also technically the first black manager in the majors, because 1962 was the year the Cubs experimented with the college of coaches, which consisted of eight coaches taking turns at managing the team, instead of having one manager.

Buck O'Neil will forever be one of the most revered figures, black or white, in all of baseball.

Considering that his last at-bat was 55 years earlier, it would have been understandable if Buck O'Neil had been a little anxious when stepping to the plate on Tuesday, July 18, 2006. But good baseball sense and plate discipline never leaves a player, not even after 55 years—not even at age 94.

On that Tuesday night, John Jordan O'Neil, known far and wide, in and out of baseball circles, as "Buck," came to bat in the first inning for the West Squad in the independent Northern League All-Star Game, making him the oldest man ever to play professional baseball. Buck was 11 years the senior of Jim Eriotes, who, one month before O'Neil, struck out in one at-bat in an independent league game in South Dakota.

O'Neil had signed a one-day contract for the express purpose of getting one at-bat in the All-Star Game to break baseball's longevity record. It was obviously a public-relations ploy for the league, but not for Buck.

"I just might take a swing at one," said the sprightly nonagenarian.

The grandson of a man brought to the United States as a slave, O'Neil was raised in Kansas City and lived there until his death on October 6, 2006. He played for and managed the Kansas City Monarchs in the Negro American League and became that city's favorite son and the unofficial mascot of the Northern League's Kansas City T-Bones.

Wearing a red and white Monarchs jersey, O'Neil led off the bottom of the first inning and took two high pitches for balls before watching a called strike. Two more balls gave O'Neil a leadoff walk, and he ambled to first base and took his lead off the bag, suggesting he might even try to steal second. He never got the chance. He was removed for a pinch runner.

When the top of the first inning ended, it was announced to the crowd that a deal had been consummated by the T-Bones to acquire O'Neil. Thus, Buck batted again in the bottom of the first inning. He took three balls and then unfurled a mighty swing at the next pitch, hoping to hit the ball over a building. He missed and spun around, almost losing his footing and falling onto the ground. But Buck maintained his balance and settled back into the batter's box to receive one more ball and his second walk of the game. A perfect night at the plate.

"This is special, very special," O'Neil said. "I've been in baseball 70 years. This is how I made my living. And here I am at 94 with a bat in my hand."

The T-Bones have campaigned vigorously to get O'Neil elected to the Baseball Hall of Fame, an honor he deserves but that has so far eluded him. To that end, at their games the T-Bones have circulated a petition throughout the stands asking baseball commissioner Bud Selig and former commissioner Fay Vincent to intervene on Buck's behalf and help him get his rightful place in baseball's pantheon of stars. At last count, they had accumulated 10,000 signatures.

"The Negro Leagues were the original independent baseball," said T-Bones owner John Ehlert, "and Buck O'Neil is the patriarch of independent baseball."

After 33 years with the Cubs, Buck left and returned "home" in 1988 as a scout for the Kansas City Royals.

In the summer of 2006, at the annual Hall of Fame induction ceremonies in Cooperstown, New York, Buck showed his class, charm, humor, good nature, warmth, and love of life and his fellow man. Seventeen players, managers, and executives from the Negro Leagues were enshrined, but O'Neil was not. He could have been bitter over the slight, but that was not Buck's style. When he was asked to deliver the keynote address at the ceremony, he gladly accepted, and he wowed the 10,000 or so spectators and the dozens of Hall of Famers and dignitaries on the dais with an eight-minute speech that displayed no recrimination, regret, or disappointment at being denied his rightful and deserving place in baseball's pantheon. The following is a selection from that speech:

This is outstanding. I've done a lot of things that I really liked doing. I hit the home run. I hit the grand-slam home run. I hit for the cycle. I've had a hole in one in golf. I've done a lot of things I liked doing. I shook hands with President Truman. Yeah! Oh, man. So I've done a lot of things I like doing, but I'd rather be right here right now, representing these people and help[ing] build a bridge across the chasm of prejudice.

This is quite an honor for me. You see, I played in the Negro Leagues. Negro Leagues baseball. All you needed was a bus—and we rode in some of the best buses money could buy—and a couple of sets of uniforms. You could have 20 of some of the best athletes who ever lived, and that's who we're representing here today.

I'm proud to have been a Negro Leagues ballplayer. They always say to me, "Buck, I know you hate people for what they did to you or what they did to your folks." I say, "No, man, I never learned to hate." I hate cancer. Cancer killed my mother. My wife died 10 years ago of cancer—I'm single, ladies. A good friend of mine died of AIDS three months ago. I hate AIDS. But I can't hate a human being because my God never made anything ugly. You can be ugly if you want to, boy, but God didn't make you that way. Uh-uh!

At that point, he asked everyone to hold hands, and he led the audience in a song of togetherness and love.

That was Buck O'Neil, a man who bore no ill will to anyone, who enjoyed life to the fullest. He was 94 years old at the time and still full of life and love.

Vic Harris was an exception among Negro Leagues players who had a tendency to jump around from team to team and even walk out on contracts when some other team offered more money. Harris spent almost his entire 28-year career with one team, the Homestead Grays, as an outstanding player and an even better manager.

Vic Harris (back row, second from right), the longtime Homestead Grays player and manager, poses with the Negro Leagues East All-Stars in 1948. *Photo courtesy of MLB Photos via Getty Images.*

Earlier I told you how hard-nosed, aggressive, and fiery Harris was as a player. Well, I have often heard that a manager manages the way he played, and that's what Harris did. He took the same traits he had as a player into the dugout as a manager. His teams played hard. They were aggressive, they were tough, and they won.

The Grays, who had earned a reputation for excellence as an independent team, joined the Negro National League in 1935. The following year, Harris took over as manager. The year after that, Harris led Homestead on a streak of nine consecutive pennants, from 1937 to 1945, during which the Grays won two consecutive Negro Leagues World Series titles, in 1943 and 1944 (under "Candy" Jim Taylor, who managed while Harris was employed in a defense plant during World War II).

Of course, it helped that Harris had players named Josh Gibson and Buck Leonard.

Athlete. Manager. Scholar. Patriot. Gentleman. Poet. Real estate broker.

Dave Malarcher was all of that.

Called "Gentleman Dave," Malarcher was genteel, cultured, educated, and soft-spoken. He never drank, never smoked, never argued with umpires, and was never ejected from a game. He adhered to the philosophy that "education should discipline the mind, and the mind should discipline the body." Malarcher was born in Louisiana the last of 10 children. His mother, who had been born into slavery, taught herself to read and write and instilled in her children the importance of education, as well as a strong work ethic and sense of decorum. Malarcher graduated from New Orleans University (now Dillard), where he starred on and captained the baseball team. After graduating from college, he played semipro baseball with the New Orleans Eagles and then joined the Indianapolis ABCs in 1916. He served in France during World War I and played baseball in the American Expeditionary Forces league.

Malarcher adhered to the philosophy that "education should discipline the mind, and the mind should discipline the body."

164

After his discharge, Malarcher joined the Detroit Stars and then the Chicago American Giants, playing under the legendary Rube Foster. A speedy, smallish (5'7", 145 pounds) switch-hitter who was a slick fielder and consistent .300 hitter, Malarcher earned a reputation as a great performer in the clutch and the Negro Leagues' premier third baseman of his day.

"Gentleman" Dave Malarcher was a well-rounded, well-loved manager who was recognized as one of the best strategists in baseball.

In 1926 Malarcher succeeded Foster as manager of the American Giants and quickly established himself as one of the game's best strategists. He won the Negro National League pennant in 1928, sat out two years, returned in 1931, and won the Negro Southern League title in 1932.

Being the diversified, well-rounded man he was, Malarcher seemed to be always drawn to pursuits other than baseball. At the age of 52, he returned to school to learn more about real estate. And he published books of poetry about a variety of subjects, including life, love, history, and baseball.

Malarcher is one guy I never met but should have. He was living in Chicago when I was playing for the New York Giants. Why I never went to meet him, I don't know, but I'm so sorry that I never met the man they called "Gentleman Dave."

Career Summaries

Manager	Years	Teams
C.I. Taylor *Led Indianapolis to a Colored Championship Series victory over Chicago American Giants in 1916*	1904–22	Birmingham Giants, West Baden Sprudels, Indianapolis ABCs
Candy Taylor *Won consecutive Negro Leagues World Series championships in 1943 and 1944*	1919–47	Dayton Marcos, Cleveland Tate Stars, Toledo Tigers, St. Louis Stars, Memphis Red Sox, Indianapolis ABCs, Detroit Stars, Nashville Elite Giants, Columbus Elite Giants, Washington Elite Giants, Chicago Giants, Homestead Grays
Buck O'Neil *Managed East-West All–Star teams from 1951 to 1954*	1948–55	Kansas City Monarchs
Vic Harris *Won seven of Grays' nine consecutive pennants from 1937 to 1945*	1936–42, 1945–47	Homestead Grays

continued	Years	Teams	
Dave Malarcher *Finished first or second every season he managed*	1926–34	Chicago American Giants	

TWELVE

Owner/Organizer/Pioneer

I could have placed Andrew "Rube" Foster on my list of the five greatest right-handed pitchers or the five greatest managers in Negro Leagues history. I chose not to for two reasons: I never saw him pitch and was not around when he managed, and his enormous contributions to Negro Leagues baseball transcend what he did on the field and in the dugout.

Rube Foster was a player, manager, owner, and commissioner; in other words, he was Cy Young, John McGraw, George Steinbrenner, and Kenesaw Mountain Landis all in one. He towered over Negro Leagues baseball, literally and figuratively.

A huge hulk of a man at 6'4" and anywhere from 220 to 260 pounds, Foster was born in Calvert, Texas, in 1879, the son of a minister who maintained his puritanical upbringing throughout his life. He never drank and never allowed alcoholic beverages in his home but bore no ill will toward those who did.

1. RUBE FOSTER

2. GUS GREENLEE

3. CUM POSEY

4. EFFA MANLEY

5. ALEX POMPEZ

Foster's leadership and organizational abilities surfaced at an early age. While he was still in grade school, he operated a baseball team in his hometown. Seduced by the game he loved and that improved with his presence—

the game that would bring him everlasting fame as "the father of Negro Leagues baseball"—Foster quit school in the eighth grade and set out to forge a career in baseball. When he was 18, he was the ace pitcher for the Waco Yellow Jackets, and he attracted attention from teams in bigger cities.

In 1902 he was invited to play with the Chicago Unions. He accepted and is said to have won 51 games for the Unions that year, including 44 in a row. In one game, he outpitched the great left-hander for the Philadelphia Athletics, Rube Waddell, after which his teammates commenced to call him "Rube," a name that stayed with him for life.

Rube Foster was a player, manager, owner, and commissioner; in other words, he was Cy Young, John McGraw, George Steinbrenner, and Kenesaw Mountain Landis all in one. He towered over Negro Leagues baseball.

Honus Wagner called Foster "one of the greatest pitchers of all time. He was the smartest pitcher I have ever seen in all my years in baseball."

Jewel Ens, a coach for the Pittsburgh Pirates, said Foster "pitched with his brains as well as his arm. He never did the wrong thing. Rube Foster would have been a sensation in the big leagues."

Rube Foster was a great pitcher and manager, but his contributions to Negro Leagues baseball were far more significant than what anybody could do on the field.

In 1907 Foster moved to the Leland Giants and became their player/manager for the next four years. In 1910 his Leland Giants posted a record of 123–6 with a team comprising some of the greatest black players of their time: Frank Wickware, Pat Dougherty, Bruce Petway, Pete Hill, John Henry "Pop" Lloyd, and "Home Run" Johnson. After the season a rift developed between Foster and Giants owner Frank C. Leland, and Rube left to establish his own team, taking Leland's best players with him.

The Chicago American Giants were born in 1911. With the White Sox of the American League moving into a brand-new stadium, Comiskey Park, Foster leased the Sox's recently vacated old stadium, South Side Park. Ever the entrepreneur, Foster began working hard to garner publicity for his new team. On afternoons of night games, he set up shop on various Chicago street corners, drumming up publicity and hawking tickets for that night's game. On one Sunday in their first season, the American Giants drew 11,000 fans, more than either the major league Cubs or White Sox.

In the 16-year period from 1911 to 1926, Foster led the American Giants to 12 championships. With the American Giants, Foster proved to be an innovative manager. He stressed pitching and defense and a racehorse offense and developed the bunt-and-run in which a player would race from first to third on a bunt.

As a manager, Foster was stern but fair. He demanded discipline but rewarded his players with season-end bonuses for jobs well done. He is said to have taught Christy Mathewson his signature pitch, the screwball or fadeaway, and was a respected and trusted friend of John McGraw's, who often visited Foster to talk baseball strategy and watch Rube's American Giants.

But playing and managing did not fulfill Foster's creative juices or his entrepreneurial aspirations. He was slated for bigger and better things, and in 1920 he embarked on an ambitious venture.

Rube Foster had a vision. It was to form a league of black baseball players that would challenge the all-white major leagues or prompt the major leagues to integrate.

Foster realized part of his vision in 1920 with the founding of the Negro National League. The caliber of play in the league was first rate, many of its players on a par with major leaguers. But the Negro National League never did present a stern challenge to the major leagues, and Foster didn't live to see integration in baseball. He served as president of the Negro National League until 1926. Shortly thereafter, Rube suffered a mental breakdown and was committed to a state institution. He died in 1930, 17 years before Jackie Robinson broke baseball's color barrier.

It was inevitable that integration would come to Major League Baseball even without Foster, but Rube probably expedited the process with his Negro National League. As a result, the Jackie Robinsons, Willie Mayses, Bob Gibsons, Roberto Clementes, Tony Gwynns, Barry Bondses, David Ortizes, and Dontrelle Willises—and the millions who thrilled to their performances on the ballfield—owe a debt of gratitude to Andrew "Rube" Foster, the father of Negro Leagues baseball.

He was known as "Mr. Big" and "King of the Hill." William Augustus "Gus" Greenlee wielded enormous power in Pittsburgh's black community and tiptoed deftly on both sides of the law.

Gus Greenlee was a bootlegger, a loan shark, and a numbers king, who, according to one report, took in between $20,000 and $25,000 per day. It was said that the Mob borrowed money from him. He was an entrepreneur and a visionary. He owned a thriving nightclub, the Crawford Grille, and a stable of fighters that included the light heavyweight champion of the world, John Henry Lewis. He built his own ballpark, and he filled it by assembling one of the greatest teams ever to play in the Negro Leagues.

Gus Greenlee had no background in baseball, as a player or otherwise, when in 1931 he decided to put together the best ballclub that money could buy. He had a buck, and he spent a buck. He wanted the best, and he was willing to pay for it, so he paid top dollar to acquire Satchel Paige, Oscar Charleston, Josh Gibson, Judy Johnson, Cool Papa Bell, Ted Page, Leroy Matlock, and Jimmie Crutchfield—all of them black baseball royalty—and made them members of his team, the Pittsburgh Crawfords.

In 1932 Gus gave his team a new home and opened Greenlee Field, the first black-owned baseball stadium. That same year, at the suggestion of one of his employees and a year before the first major league All-Star Game, Greenlee conceived the Negro Leagues All-Star Game and promoted the first one in 1933.

For two years, Greenlee's Crawfords dominated black baseball, taking on and beating all comers. With no more worlds to conquer, Greenlee decided to form his own league, the Negro National League. It had six charter members, the Crawfords, Homestead Grays, Chicago American Giants, Indianapolis ABCs, Detroit Stars, and Columbus Blue Birds, and it was presided over by—who else?—Gus Greenlee.

Gus Greenlee had no baseball background to speak of when he started the Pittsburgh Crawfords ballclub, which dominated the Negro Leagues for years. *Photo courtesy of the Negro Leagues Baseball Museum.*

As league president, Greenlee ruled with an iron fist and complete autonomy. By the end of the first half of the split season, the Homestead Grays and Indianapolis ABCs were drummed out of the league—charged with raiding other teams for players—and replaced by the Nashville Elite Giants and Baltimore Black Sox.

The American Giants had edged the Crawfords by one game for the first-half championship. The second-half schedule was never completed, records were expunged, and the Giants, as first-half winner, logically claimed the league championship.

But logic had no place in Gus Greenlee's world. As league president, he arbitrarily announced that the American Giants had not won the championship. Instead, he awarded it to his own Crawfords. No reason was given. Gus didn't need one. And no other team owner objected to his decision or challenged his authority.

I knew Gus Greenlee, and I liked him very much. He was the nicest guy in the world. I know he took from the community with his numbers racket, but he gave back to the community, too. He never reneged on a payoff, and he was a soft touch for any sob story, always willing to help out and support members of his community who had a valid need or a worthwhile endeavor.

His Crawford Grille was the center of entertainment in Pittsburgh's hill section, and Gus had a monopoly on the residents' entertainment dollar. When the Crawfords played, fans would go to his club to eat and drink before the game, then go to Greenlee Stadium for the game, and return to the Crawford Grille after the game. His club got to be so popular that he opened a second place, Crawford Grille II.

Not only did Gus pay his players top dollar, but he also treated them well. His team traveled first class and played in a new state-of-the-art stadium, and he handed out bonuses at the end of the season for outstanding play.

Rube Foster was "the father of Negro Leagues baseball," but in his own way, Gus Greenlee was as much a patriarch as Foster.

After Rube Foster, and before Gus Greenlee made the scene, the strongman of Negro baseball was Cumberland Willis "Cum" Posey, who rose up the ladder from player to manager to owner and built the Homestead Grays into a powerhouse.

Cum Posey was born in Homestead, Pennsylvania, a suburb of Pittsburgh. Like George Steinbrenner, Cum was the son of a wealthy shipping magnate who also was a part owner of a newspaper, *The Pittsburgh Courier*. An outstanding basketball player, he made a name for himself in basketball first at Duquesne University and then at Penn State. He joined the Murdock Grays as an outfielder in 1911, the year before they became the Homestead Grays.

Posey was just a mediocre player, but he showed that he had a great baseball mind and was named manager of the Grays in 1916. Despite losing his best players—Josh Gibson, Oscar Charleston, Judy Johnson, and Ted Page—to Gus Greenlee's bottomless bankroll, Posey rebuilt the Grays into a top team in the East and the dominant team in the second Negro National League.

Like Rube Foster before him, Posey's ambitions extended beyond the playing field and dugout, so he assumed ownership of the Grays.

In 1937 Posey formed an alliance with Clark Griffith, owner of the Washington Senators, and arranged to have the Grays play their home games in Washington's Griffith Stadium.

Cum Posey was an average player on the field, but as a manager and later the team's owner, he rebuilt the Homestead Grays into one of the dominant teams of the era.

175

Like many of his contemporaries, Posey's dream was the integration of Major League Baseball. He lived long enough to see Jackie Robinson and his own pitcher, John Wright, sign with the Brooklyn Dodgers in 1946 but never got to see them play on a white team. Posey died on March 28, 1946, a week before Robinson and Wright made their debut as members of the International League's Montreal Royals.

Decades before Joan Payson with the New York Mets, Joan Kroc in San Diego, and Marge Schott in Cincinnati, **Effa Manley** was "the first lady of baseball."

As a pioneer, an innovator, and a champion of women's rights, Effa was years—no, decades—ahead of her time. My boss with the Newark Eagles was a business genius, had a gift for publicity, was at the forefront of the civil rights movement, and fought for the equality of women in management positions long before it was fashionable to do so.

She has been called "the Queen of the Negro Leagues," and that's a fitting description because Effa Manley was a queen in every respect. She was the first

Effa Manley, a real visionary and the first female elected into the Baseball Hall of Fame, was truly the "first woman of baseball."

woman owner of a baseball team, the only woman owner of a Negro Leagues team, and the first woman elected to the Baseball Hall of Fame, in 2006.

On her Hall of Fame plaque it says: "A trailblazing owner and tireless crusader in the civil rights movement who earned the respect of her players and fellow owners. As business manager and co-owner of the Eagles, ensured team's financial success with creative promotions and advertising. Beloved by fans because she integrated her players into the community and fielded consistently competitive teams, highlighted by 1946 Negro Leagues World Series championship."

I have nothing but good things to say about Mrs. Manley, and I concur with what's written on her plaque. She was very civic-minded, and she was beloved in Newark. The citizens liked her very much, and she supported the city financially.

She did a lot of good things that she didn't get credit for. She would tell us, "Whether you guys know it or not, you're role models. Conduct yourselves properly and dress well. Mind your p's and q's." She would give us as much money as she possibly could.

Mrs. Manley was born Effa Brooks in Philadelphia, but she moved to New York after graduating from high school and worked in the millinery business. She met Abe Manley at, of all places, Yankee Stadium during the 1932 World Series.

"Babe Ruth made a baseball fan of me," Mrs. Manley once said. "I used to go to Yankee Stadium just to see him come to bat."

Abe Manley was a wealthy businessman who made his fortune either through real estate investments or in the numbers racket, depending on which story you believe.

Through the years, there has been much controversy over Effa's ethnicity. Beautiful and fair-skinned, she could pass for white—and often did—but she preferred to live her life as a black woman. Effa's mother was of German and Asian-Indian descent and her stepfather black, and she was raised as a black woman with black half siblings.

Effa and Abe were married in 1935. Soon after their wedding, Abe, who followed Negro Leagues teams on barnstorming tours, decided to start his own team. He formed the Brooklyn Eagles and arranged to have their games played in Ebbets Field, home of the Dodgers.

Abe taught Effa baseball, and she joined her husband in the venture. With her love for baseball and her business acumen, she and Abe had an ideal union. Eventually, Effa took over the operation of every facet of the club.

"Abe and I had a magnificent partnership," Mrs. Manley once said. "He put the club together, and I took care of the business details."

Among Mrs. Manley's duties was drumming up publicity for the Eagles. For their inaugural game, she succeeded in getting New York City Mayor Fiorello LaGuardia to throw out the first ball and had more than 185 VIPs, including New York State Supreme Court Justice Charles C. Lockwood, on hand for the Eagles' first game. Unfortunately, the Kansas City Monarchs crushed the Eagles, 21–7. Mrs. Manley was especially devastated and embarrassed by the defeat.

"She left the ballpark," remembered first baseman George Giles. "When she was displeased, the world came to an end. She'd stop traffic. Mrs. Manley loved baseball, but she couldn't stand to lose. I was a pretty hard loser myself, but I think she'd take it more seriously than anybody."

Before long, Abe was turning over more and more of the day-to-day operation of the team to his wife, who arranged playing schedules, booked travel, managed the payroll, bought equipment, and negotiated contracts in addition to handling publicity and promotions. Effa thrived in her role as a club owner, even to the point of getting involved in on-field decisions. When the Eagles suffered through a losing record in their first year, Mrs. Manley insisted that Manager Ben Taylor be fired and replaced by Giles. It was Abe who approached Giles and told him, "My wife wants you to manage the ball-club."

There was a story that one time Mrs. Manley demanded that Terris McDuffie be the starting pitcher for a game because she wanted to show him off to members of her social club, and another story had her giving signs to players by crossing and uncrossing her legs.

The Manleys quickly realized that trying to compete with the Dodgers in Brooklyn for fans was a losing proposition, and, in 1936, they moved the team to Newark, where the Eagles soon became a vital part of the community and a valuable resource of the city. Effa was active in Newark's civic causes and a constant presence at many political, business, and social gatherings as a means of promoting her baseball team and furthering her interest in causes. She was an outspoken activist and crusader for black civil rights, serving as treasurer of the Newark chapter of the NAACP and as a member of the Citizens' League for Fair Play.

In 1934 she organized a boycott of Harlem stores that refused to hire black salesclerks. As a result of her efforts, stores on 125th Street hired 300 black workers.

In 1939 she staged an antilynching day at an Eagles game in Ruppert Stadium.

All the while, Effa was maternal toward her players. In 1946 the Eagles provided a $15,000 air-conditioned Flexible Clipper bus for travel, a first for a Negro Leagues team. Concerned that their players would have no income during the off-season, the Manleys sponsored a team made up mainly of Eagles in the Puerto Rican Winter League.

The Manleys helped Lenny Pearson get started in the tavern business, advanced me a loan for a down payment on my first house, and served as god-parents to Larry Doby's daughter.

Effa was a woman who believed in standing up for her rights. At league meetings, she was outspoken, forceful, and demanding, which miffed many of her male counterparts. But they respected her, and they listened to her. She also had the courage to stand up to Branch Rickey, a powerful man in Major League Baseball.

Rickey signed several players from the Negro Leagues, including Jackie Robinson, Dan Bankhead, Roy Campanella, Joe Black, Sam Jethroe, and Jim Gilliam, and he never paid the Negro Leagues owners a penny. They would ask him, "Aren't you going to give us some money?" and Rickey's response was, "The contracts are not valid, so I don't have to pay you anything."

Rickey took Don Newcombe from the Eagles and signed me to a contract, but, as I explained earlier, I didn't feel I was ready, so I stayed with the Eagles. Later, when the New York Giants wanted to sign me, I wrote to the Dodgers and told them I had this opportunity and asked them to release me. Rickey wrote back and said, "You still belong to us."

That's when Mrs. Manley got into it. She told Rickey, "You didn't give us any money for Newcombe; I want at least $5,000 for Monte."

Again, Rickey said no money, and Mrs. Manley called his bluff. She said, "If you don't give us any money, I'm going to sue you."

Rather than get involved in a lawsuit, which would bring him bad publicity, Rickey backed down and released me. Horace Stoneham gave the Eagles $5,000, and I signed with the Giants.

It was through Mrs. Manley's efforts, and her courage to stand up to Rickey, that Negro Leagues owners began to be compensated when their players were signed by the major leagues. When Bill Veeck wanted to sign Larry Doby for his Cleveland Indians, Mrs. Manley asked him for $5,000, and Veeck said, "If he makes our ballclub, I'll give you $15,000," and that's what he did.

There were two sides to this story. Although Negro Leagues owners were getting paid for their players, it was the beginning of the end of Negro Leagues baseball. All the good players were being signed by the major leagues, and the black fans that supported the Negro Leagues teams started going to major league games to see the stars they used to see in the Negro Leagues. As a result, the Newark Eagles, who once outdrew even the Newark Bears of the International League, saw their attendance begin to decline dramatically, and in 1947, the Manleys sold the team to a black dentist in Memphis, Tennessee. A year later, the team folded.

After she left baseball, Mrs. Manley had a new cause to occupy her time. She devoted herself to keeping the history of Negro Leagues baseball alive and campaigned for recognition of Negro Leagues teams and great players by way of election to the Hall of Fame in Cooperstown. It came to pass in 1973.

179

Mrs. Manley died in 1981 at the age of 81. She's buried in Holy Cross Cemetery in Culver City, California. Her gravestone reads, "She loved baseball."

I was playing in Puerto Rico in the winter of 1948–49 when **Alex Pompez** approached me. I knew Alex as the owner of the New York Cubans, an outstanding team in the Negro National League.

He was born Alejandro Pompez in Key West, Florida, the son of Cuban immigrants, and he inherited from his parents' homeland an abiding love for baseball.

Alex had made a bundle of money in the numbers business. His partner was one of the big-time racketeers—Dutch Schultz I believe—and they had a big hit on one number that they couldn't pay off, so Alex fled to Mexico for two years until he could build back his bankroll. He returned to the United States and built the Cubans into a Negro Leagues powerhouse.

Alex was a lovely man, the nicest guy in the world. He had a sense of humor, and he always wanted to do the right thing. He loved the dollar, sure, but if he made a buck, he made sure his players were taken care of. He always tried to get as much money for the players as he could. He got along with everybody, Cuban players, black players. Everybody loved him. He married the sister of Senator Edward Brooke of Massachusetts, and they were a very, very happy couple.

When the Negro Leagues began to crumble after the integration of the major leagues, Pompez became a scout for the New York Giants and was instrumental in the Giants signing such Latin American players as Orlando Cepeda, Juan Marichal, the Alou brothers, Ruben Gomez, and Ray Noble.

It was Alex Pompez—a man I liked, respected, and trusted—who approached me in Puerto Rico.

"How would you like to play for the New York Giants?" Pompez asked me.

Of course I said I would, but I warned him that I had signed a contract with the Dodgers and that could be a problem. That's when I wrote to the Dodgers and tried to get my release, but they refused. That's when Mrs. Manley got into it and threatened to sue the Dodgers and they gave me my release, and Horace Stoneham paid the Eagles $5,000 for my contract.

Alex Pompez was universally loved in baseball circles and, after becoming a scout for the New York Giants, was instrumental in getting me into the major leagues.

As a result, everybody was happy, except Branch Rickey and the Brooklyn Dodgers. The Manleys got the $5,000, the New York Giants got themselves a ballplayer, and I got my chance to play in the major leagues, all because of Alex Pompez.

At Pompez's posthumous and long overdue induction into the Hall of Fame in Cooperstown in the summer of 2006, Juan Marichal said Pompez was "like a father to us all."

Orlando Cepeda added, "When I went to my first Giants tryout camp with [Willie] McCovey and Jose Pagan in Melbourne, Florida, in 1955, we got off at the Greyhound bus station, and no cabbies would take us to the camp. A call was put in to Pompez, and he came and got us, took us to our barracks, and basically took care of us the rest of the time.

That's the Alex Pompez I knew and loved. He was just a wonderful man.

Career Summaries

Name	Years	Teams
Rube Foster	1911–26	Chicago American Giants, Negro National League (founder)
Gus Greenlee	1931–36	Pittsburgh Crawfords
Cum Posey	1911–46	Homestead Grays, Detroit Wolves, East-West League (founder)
Effa Manley	1935–48	Brooklyn Eagles, Newark Eagles
Alex Pompez	1922–50	Cuban Stars, New York Cubans

THIRTEEN

Team

Start with the greatest slugger in Negro Leagues baseball history—maybe the greatest slugger in the history of all baseball, black or white—Josh Gibson, the so-called Black Babe Ruth. Add Oscar Charleston, the man regarded as the league's best all-around player, its finest third baseman, the fastest man ever to wear a pair of spiked shoes, and a dominant pitcher who also happened to be the league's most charismatic player and its greatest attraction, and what do you have? The Negro Leagues' greatest team, the **Pittsburgh Crawfords**, which got its name from a nightclub, or vice versa.

Which came first, the chicken or the egg? Gus Greenlee's Crawford Grille or his Pittsburgh Crawfords? History tells us that there was a popular semipro baseball team called the Crawfords in Pittsburgh in 1928–29 that featured a young slugger named

1. PITTSBURGH CRAWFORDS

2. HOMESTEAD GRAYS

3. KANSAS CITY MONARCHS

4. NEWARK EAGLES

5. NEW YORK CUBANS

Josh Gibson and that Greenlee, a numbers boss and king of "the Hill" (a section of Pittsburgh), owned a popular nightspot he called the Crawford Grille. It is thought that in 1931, when he decided to organize a team and enter it in the Negro National League, he borrowed the name *Crawfords* from the semi-pro team and his own nightclub.

In putting together his team, Greenlee spared no expense. He paid top dollar to lure from other teams Josh Gibson, already a local favorite; Oscar Charleston; Judy Johnson, the league's premier third baseman; Cool Papa Bell, the fastest man in spiked shoes; and the redoubtable Satchel Paige, a dominant pitcher and the league's most charismatic player and greatest attraction. All five were elected to the Hall of Fame.

In supporting roles were Jud Wilson, another Hall of Famer; Rap Dixon; and Ted "Double Duty" Radcliffe. (Damon Runyon pinned that nickname on Radcliffe during the 1932 Negro Leagues World Series when, in a doubleheader, Radcliffe caught Satchel Paige's shutout in the first game and

This 1935 Pittsburgh Crawfords team is widely considered one of the greatest baseball teams ever assembled.

pitched a shutout of his own in the second game. Wrote Runyon, "Radcliffe is worth the price of two admissions.") Joining Bell in the outfield were Jimmie Crutchfield and Sam Bankhead, forming what many consider baseball's fastest outfield.

A poster promoting the Crawfords' visit to the nation's capitol for a three-game series against the Washington Pilots advertised the Crawfords as featuring "Oscar Charleston The Great One Hand First Baseman" and "Satchell [sic] Paige The Canon ball pitcher."

For five years, from 1932 to 1936, the Crawfords dominated play in Negro Leagues baseball, particularly the team's 1935 edition, which many have called the greatest black baseball team of all time. They won the first-half title by seven games over the Columbus Elite Giants with a record of 26–6, a phenomenal .785 winning percentage, but in the second half, they finished second to the New York Cubans.

In a seven-game playoff for the league championship, the Crawfords defeated the Cubans, four games to three.

In 1936 the Crawfords were touched by controversy when they were falsely accused of throwing a game against the Bushwicks, a powerful New York semipro team. Although the Crawfords were absolved of any wrongdoing, the accusations stayed with them and tainted their image.

A year later, Greenlee, who lived by the sword, died by the sword when Santo Domingo dictator Rafael Trujillo came calling on the Crawfords and outbid Greenlee for the services of several members of the team, including Gibson, Paige, and Bell.

The Crawfords' dominance had come to an end, and they would never be the same. In 1939 Greenlee sold the team, the Crawfords moved to Toledo, and a magical era in Negro Leagues baseball had come to an abrupt close.

It's quite amazing to think that at one time Pittsburgh and its environs were home to what in my opinion are the two greatest teams in Negro Leagues history, the Crawfords in the Hill section of the city and the Grays in Homestead, a suburb about 20 miles southeast of the city. Add the Pirates, a consistent National League contender with such stars as Pie Traynor, the Waner Brothers (Paul and Lloyd), and Arky Vaughan, all Hall of Famers, and the city of Pittsburgh in the 1930s could rival New York as the baseball capital of the world.

With the Grays in Homestead and the Crawfords and MLB Pirates both in the city, Pittsburgh rivaled New York as the baseball capital of the world throughout the 1930s.

The **Homestead Grays** were formed in 1910 as a weekend recreational team comprising workers at the U.S. Steel factory in Homestead. Two years later, a young outfielder named Cum Posey joined the team. Posey was only a mediocre player, but he was a man with a vision, eventually taking over ownership of the Grays and building them into what would become, with the possible exception of the Kansas City Monarchs, the most successful and best-known team in the history of Negro Leagues baseball.

Posey also built the Grays into a dynasty. In the 1930s and 1940s, they won nine consecutive Negro National League pennants, and the 1938 team has often been called the greatest Negro Leagues team ever assembled, a murderers' row led by Josh Gibson (strange how great teams just kept following him around) and Buck Leonard. Considered the equal of Babe Ruth and Lou Gehrig as a one-two power punch, they were dubbed by the press the "Thunder Twins" and the "Dynamite Twins."

Starting in the late 1930s, Posey arranged for the Grays to play a portion of their home games in Washington, D.C., at Griffith Stadium, home of the hapless Washington Senators, whom the Grays regularly outdrew.

It was there that Senators owner Clark Griffith, watching Grays games from his office, saw Gibson and Leonard bomb prodigious home runs and salivated at the thought of these "Thunder Twins" turning his ragtag team into contenders in the American League. Griffith toyed with the idea of signing Gibson and Leonard to contracts and breaking the Major League color barrier, but in the end he admitted he lacked the courage to take such a bold step.

Negro Leagues owners had one great advantage over their major league brethren: they were unencumbered by a reserve clause that bound a player in perpetuity to the team that held his contract. And Negro Leagues owners had one other advantage over the major leaguers. Players' contracts were unenforceable, either because the owners wouldn't, or couldn't, file suit against them for breach of contract.

Negro Leagues players had a tendency to recklessly jump contracts and, without fear of punishment, sign with another team that would pay them more money. As a result, any owner with deep pockets who was willing to loosen his purse strings could put together a powerhouse team.

One such owner was a white man, James Leslie (more commonly known as J.L.) Wilkinson of the **Kansas City Monarchs**, the most famous, most popular, and longest running franchise in Negro Leagues history. Decades before George Steinbrenner used free agency, and his checkbook, to rebuild the New York Yankees into another dynasty, Wilkinson used his seemingly inexhaustible financial resources to assemble "the best team money could buy" in Negro Leagues baseball.

At one time or another, 11 of the 30 players elected to the Negro Leagues wing of the Baseball Hall of Fame—Cool Papa Bell, Willard Brown, Andy Cooper, Willie Foster, Jose Mendez, Satchel Paige, "Bullet" Joe Rogan, Hilton Smith, Turkey Stearnes, Cristóbal Torriente, and Willie Wells—wore the uniform of the Kansas City Monarchs. This list does not include former Monarchs Jackie Robinson and Ernie Banks, who were voted into the Hall of Fame as major leaguers. The Monarchs also sent more than 20 players to the major leagues, more than any other Negro Leagues team.

Born in Iowa, Wilkinson was a promising pitcher until he hurt his arm and became a baseball entrepreneur and innovator. He developed the first

Long before George Steinbrenner's New York Yankees were dubbed the best team money can buy, there was J.L. Wilkinson and his Kansas City Monarchs.

successful portable lighting system for night games and trucked it along with the Monarchs on barnstorming tours, formed a traveling women's baseball team, and organized the All-Nations team, which was made up of black, white, and Native American players.

The Monarchs won three consecutive pennants, from 1923 to 1925, and the first Negro Leagues World Series, in 1924. When the Negro American League was formed in 1937, the Monarchs ran off six more pennants in seven years and capped it off in the 1942 World Series with a four-game sweep of the Homestead Grays of Josh Gibson and Buck Leonard.

In all, the Monarchs won 17 pennants and two World Series.

I'll admit to a little prejudice in picking the **Newark Eagles** as the fourth-greatest team in the Negro Leagues—but only a little. I honestly believe that the team I played with for 11 seasons—the only Negro Leagues team I ever played with—stacks up favorably with any team in the history of black baseball.

Among the all-time greats that played for the Eagles were Ray Dandridge, Willie Wells, Leon Day, and Mule Suttles.

The 1946 team, with a double-play combination of Doby at second base and Irvin at shortstop—that's right, Larry Doby, the future Cleveland Indians All-Star center fielder at second, and yours truly at short—finished first in both halves of the Negro National League season. We beat the Philadelphia Stars by five and a half games in the first half and the New York Cubans by four games in the second half and then upset the heavily favored Kansas City Monarchs of the Negro American League in the World Series, four games to three.

It's only fair that I mention that Satchel Paige was supposed to pitch the seventh game for the Monarchs, but for some reason he didn't show up. Instead, they started Ford Smith, and he pitched a terrific game and held us to just two hits, but we won the game, 3–2. It was my good fortune to score the winning run and to be named World Series Most Valuable Player.

I have always wondered if we would have beaten Satchel. At the same time, I was so confident in the ability of my teammates, I think we could have beaten any pitcher that day. But we'll never know for sure.

I thought we had the makings of a dynasty in Newark, but two things happened. First, Abe and Effa Manley, the husband and wife who owned the team, let Wells, Dandridge, Suttles, and Day get away. I thought that was a mistake. We were young, we were winning, and we were drawing fans. They should have kept that good team together. They should have paid Dandridge, Wells, and Suttles enough money that they wouldn't jump to other teams. They could have kept a good team there. We were drawing like crazy in Newark. At one point, we even outdrew the Bears of the International League at a time when the Bears, a farm team of the New York Yankees', were being hailed as the greatest minor league team ever. But if a player left the Eagles to play for more money elsewhere, the Manleys would let him walk and look for somebody they could sign a little cheaper to replace him.

The second thing that happened was progress. The major leagues integrated the year after we won the Negro Leagues championship, and three of us—Doby, Don Newcombe, and I—who never had played with another Negro Leagues team, got our big break and signed major league contracts.

The 1938 Newark Eagles. That's me (bottom row, second from left) as an 18-year-old rookie. In the top row, from left to right, are Mule Suttles, Willie Wells, Bob Evans, Max Manning, Red Moore, Len Pearson, and Ed Stone. In the bottom row, from left, are Leon Day, me, Dick Lundy, John Hayes, and Dick Seay. *Photo courtesy of Bettmann/CORBIS.*

Eventually the inevitable, the thing I feared, happened. As the major leagues siphoned away the best players from the Negro Leagues, the Eagles, and the rest of the black teams, vanished.

Their run of success wasn't very long, but for a short time Alex Pompez's **New York Cubans** were a powerhouse in the Negro National League.

One man was mostly responsible for much of their success on the field: Martin Dihigo, the Cuban who played all nine positions and played them well. There are many who say Dihigo was the greatest player ever to play in the Negro Leagues. Without question, he was the most versatile.

Negro Leaguers in the Hall of Fame

Name	Year Inducted	Position
Cool Papa Bell	1974	OF, P
Ray Brown	2006	P
Willard Brown	2006	OF, SS
Oscar Charleston	1976	OF, 1B, MGR
Andy Cooper	2006	P, MGR
Ray Dandridge	1987	3B, SS, 2B
Leon Day	1995	P
Martin Dihigo	1977	P, OF, 1B, 2B, SS, 3B, C, MGR
Rube Foster	1981	Pioneer/Executive
Willie Foster	1996	P, MGR
Josh Gibson	1972	C, OF
Frank Grant	2006	2B, SS
Pete Hill	2006	OF, 2B, MGR
Monte Irvin	1973	OF, SS, 3B
Judy Johnson	1975	3B, SS, MGR
Buck Leonard	1972	1B, OF
Pop Lloyd	1977	SS, 1B, 2B, C, MGR
Biz Mackey	2006	C, SS, MGR
Effa Manley	2006	Pioneer/Executive
Jose Mendez	2006	P, SS, 3B, 2B, MGR
Satchel Paige	1971	P
Alex Pompez	2006	Pioneer/Executive
Cum Posey	2006	Pioneer/Executive
"Bullet" Joe Rogan	1998	P, OF, 1B, 2B, 3B, SS, MGR
Louis Santop	2006	C, OF
Hilton Smith	2001	P
Turkey Stearnes	2000	OF
Mule Suttles	2006	1B, OF
Ben Taylor	2006	1B, MGR

Cristóbal Torriente	2006	OF, P
Willie Wells	1997	SS, 3B, MGR
Sol White	2006	Pioneer/Executive
J.L. Wilkinson	2006	Pioneer/Executive
"Smokey" Joe Williams	1999	P, MGR
Jud Wilson	2006	3B, 1B, MGR

Although the great Dihigo had retired by 1947, the Cubans still had a formidable team and continued to win without their big star. They won the Negro National League pennant and then defeated the Cleveland Buckeyes in the World Series, four games to one. Leading the offense was a young Cuban who would go on to become an outstanding major leaguer and one of the most colorful, enduring, and ageless players ever. His name was Orestes "Minnie" Minoso.

Also on the Cubans' 1947 championship team was a Cuban pitcher named Luis Tiant—no, not the wonderfully inventive and deceptive Looey who was the ace of the Boston Red Sox pitching staff in the 1970s. This pitcher was his father, Luis Tiant Sr., a crafty, junk-balling left-hander, who had a great move to first base. If you got off the base even a couple of inches, you were in trouble. When Tiant was doing his thing, you couldn't tell if he was going home or throwing to first base.

I hadn't seen him in a while, and one day another player asked me, "Monte, have you seen Tiant lately?" I said I hadn't, and this player said, "Let me tell you how good his move to first base is. I was hitting against him in one game and he went into his stretch and he did his thing and threw over to first base. But his move was so good, when he threw to first I swung. I argued like hell with the umpire that I foul tipped it."

I saw Luis Jr. a short time ago, and I told him that story. Looey said, "He was a left-hander. I'm a right-hander; I didn't have that kind of move."

Historians are sure to notice, and point out, that I have not included among my five greatest teams Rube Foster's Chicago American Giants, who dominated in the dark ages of Negro Leagues baseball, the 1910s and 1920s. There's no doubt they belong, but because I never saw them, I don't feel qualified to rate them.

I have restricted my selections of the greatest teams to those I saw or played with or against. Following are some teams I saw who came close to being

The 1921 New York Cubans pose with owner Alex Pompez (back row, fifth from left), who built the franchise into a power.

rated in the top five but just failed to make the cut. They are listed alphabetically, not in order of preference.

Baltimore Elite Giants—They won the Negro National League title in 1939 with Biz Mackey and Roy Campanella, and in 1949 with Joe Black and Jim Gilliam.

Birmingham Black Barons—They had Piper Davis, Pepper Bassett, Artie Wilson, and Sam Hairston. In 1948 the Barons won the Negro American League championship with a 17-year-old center fielder named Willie Mays.

Detroit Stars—A charter member of the Negro National League, the team's top players were Pete Hill, Turkey Stearnes, and catcher Bruce Petway, who twice threw out Ty Cobb attempting to steal in a game in Cuba.

Indianapolis ABCs—I didn't see them until the 1930s. Before then, they had such stars as Oscar Charleston, Bingo DeMoss, Biz Mackey, Ben Taylor, and Cannonball Redding.

Indianapolis Clowns—This team launched the baseball career of Hank Aaron. Major leaguers Choo Choo Coleman, John Wyatt, and Paul Casanova also played for the Clowns, who were best known, as their name implies, for their antics on the field, much like the Harlem Globetrotters are known in basketball. In fact, Goose Tatum, the 'Trotters' master showman, also played for the Clowns. Goose was a pretty good first baseman, but his greatest value was in his antics that never failed to break up audiences wherever the Clowns played.

Memphis Red Sox—Their alumni include major leaguers Dan Bankhead, Bob Boyd, Marshall Bridges, and Charlie Pride, who gave up a promising baseball career to become a star as a country-and-western singer.

New York Black Yankees—They're best known for their co-owner, the great tap dancer Bill "Bojangles" Robinson, a bigger star than any of his players.

Team Summaries

Team	Years
Pittsburgh Crawfords *Key players: Paige, Gibson, Charleston, Bell*	1931–38
Homestead Grays *Key players: Gibson, Leonard*	1910–50
Kansas City Monarchs *Key players: Bell, Paige, Foster, Stearnes*	1915–55
Newark Eagles *Key players: Dandridge, Suttles, Wells, Day*	1936–48
New York Cubans *Key players: Dihigo, Dandridge, Lundy*	1935–50

Bibliography

Feller, Bob, with Bill Gilbert. *Now Pitching: Bob Feller*. New York: Birch Lane Press, 1990.

Hogan, Lawrence D. *Shades of Glory*. Washington, D.C.: National Geographic, 2006.

Kuhn, Bowie. *Hardball: The Education of a Baseball Commissioner*. New York: Times Books, 1987.

Monteleone, John J. *Branch Rickey's Little Blue Book*. New York: Macmillan, 1995.

Paige, LeRoy (Satchel), as told to David Lipman. *Maybe I'll Pitch Forever*. New York: Zebra Books, 1961.

Peterson, Robert. *Only the Ball Was White*. Englewood Cliffs, NJ: Prentice Hall, 1970.

Robinson, Jackie. *Baseball Has Done It*. New York: Lippincott, 1964.

Index

Entries in italics denote references to photo captions.

JOSH GIBSON • ROY CAMPANELLA • BIZ MACKEY •
GEORGE GILES • MULE SUTTLES • LUKE EASTER • BO
ALLEN • JIM GILLIAM • PIPER DAVIS • WILLIE WELL
BECKWITH • RAY DANDRIDGE • JUDY JOHNSON • OLI
ROBINSON • MINNIE MINOSO • VIC HARRIS • SANI
CHARLESTON • COOL PAPA BELL • LARRY DOBY
TORRIENTE • BILL WRIGHT • SAM JETHROE • JIMMIE
• LEON DAY • BULLET JOE ROGAN • MARTIN DIHIGO
DONALDSON • BARNEY BROWN • C.I. TAYLOR •
MALARCHER • RUBE FOSTER • GUS GREENLEE • CUM
ROY CAMPANELLA • BIZ MACKEY • LOUIS SANTOP •
MULE SUTTLES • LUKE EASTER • BOB BOYD • JACK
GILLIAM • PIPER DAVIS • WILLIE WELLS • POP LLOYD
DANDRIDGE • JUDY JOHNSON • OLIVER MARCELLE
MINNIE MINOSO • VIC HARRIS • SANDY AMOROS • W
COOL PAPA BELL • LARRY DOBY • TURKEY STEAR
WRIGHT • SAM JETHROE • JIMMIE CRUTCHFIELD •
BULLET JOE ROGAN • MARTIN DIHIGO • WILLIE FOST
BARNEY BROWN • C.I. TAYLOR • CANDY TAYLOR •